Essential Series

Springer

London
Berlin
Heidelberg
New York
Barcelona
Hong Kong
Milan
Paris
Santa Clara
Singapore
Tokyo

John Cowell

Essential Visual
J++ 6.0 *fast*

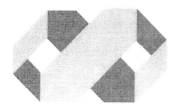

How to develop Java
applications and applets with
Visual J++

Springer

Author and Series Editor

John Cowell, BSc (Hons), MPhil, PhD
Department of Computer and Information Sciences
De Montfort University, Kents Hill Campus,
Hammerwood Gate, Kents Hill, Milton Keynes, MK7 6HP, UK

ISBN 1-85233-013-9 Springer-Verlag London Berlin Heidelberg

British Library Cataloguing in Publication Data
Cowell, John, 1957 -
    Essential Visual Basic J++ 6.0 fast: : how to develop Java Applications and
    applets with Visual J++. (Essential series)
    1. Java (Computer program language) 2. Visual programming (Computer science)
    I. Title II. Visual J++ fast
    005.1'33
ISBN 1852330139

Library of Congress Cataloging-in-Publication Data
Cowell, John. 1957-
    Essential Visual J++ 6.0 Fast : how to develop Java applications and
    applets with Visual J++ / John Cowell.
        p.   cm.
    Includes index
    ISBN 1-85233-013-9 (alk. paper)
    1. Microsoft Visual J++. 2. Java (Computer program language)
I. Title
QA76.73.J38C695 1998
005.2'762 -- DC21   98-7024

Microsoft, MS, Visual Basic, Visual J++, Windows, Windows 95 and Windows 98 are trademarks of Microsoft Corporation Ltd.
Delphi, Open Jbuilder are trademarks of Borland Corporation Ltd.
Java and Hot Java are trademarks of Sun Microsystems Corporation Ltd.
Pentium is a trademark of Intel Corporation Ltd.

Typesetting: Camera-ready by author
Printed and bound by Athenæum Press, Gateshead, Tyne & Wear
34/3830-54321   Printed on acid-free paper SPIN 10792439

Contents

1
Why Use Visual J++?

Introduction

When Sun first released Java, few people could have guessed that it would quickly have become one of the most popular programming languages in the world. Java is the only language you can use to create WORA (write once run anywhere) applications and applets which can be run on any type of computer. Applets are applications written in Java which can run within a browser environment such as Internet Explorer. They allow you to create dynamic interactive Web pages for the Internet.

The Internet, and particularly the World Wide Web, is now used by over 100 million people world-wide with every type of computer system. Pages for the Web are written in HTML (Hypertext Markup Language), which allows you to control the content and appearance of the page and to have links to other pages. The great thing about HTML is that it can be understood by any computer provided that the computer has a browser, such as MS Internet Explorer or Netscape. Static HTML has some important limitations, you cannot use it to do a lot of processing of information and it has limited capabilities for handling graphics. If you want to write an on-line help system, HTML would be a good choice, but if you want to write a serious application for managing accounts with a Windows-style user interface you need to use a language such as Visual C++, Delphi, or Visual Basic. Using these languages to write your programs is fine providing everyone who wants to use it has a PC.

Using Java you can write an application or applet which will run within a Virtual Java machine environment on any computer. If your favourite word processor or spread sheet was written in Java you could run it on a PC, Apple Mac, or Sun workstation without making any changes whatsoever. This has enormous benefits for users and programmers.

Sun Microsystems helped Java to become popular by making it available from their web site for free. It was downloaded to computers over the world and its potential was quickly realised. The Sun toolkit gave you everything you needed to write Java applications and applets, but to programmers used to powerful IDEs (Integrated Development Environments) such as Visual Basic it was clear that Java needed its own IDE. Visual J++ is the environment that Java programmers have been waiting for.

1

What this book covers

Java is an object oriented language and programmers who know languages such as Pascal often find this the most difficult aspect of the language. This book discusses the key concepts of object orientation and uses many examples at every stage to show how you can write Java applets and applications fast.

If you have used a range of Windows software, but do not have a strong programming background, you will find all you need in this book to write serious applications and applets.

If you are an experienced programmer and have used Windows IDE such as Visual Basic, you will find that this will help you to make the transition to Visual J++.

If you are a Java programmer who does not know the Visual J++ environment you will find this book useful in understanding how Java has been integrated into the environment. Visual J++ can greatly improve the productivity of Java programmers who are still using the free Sun toolkit.

One of the great benefits of object orientation is that you can use existing classes to build complex applications and applets rather than re-writing the same code every time. The capabilities of the Java language is greatly increased by a powerful API (Application Programming Interface). This book covers the key aspects of the extensive Java API classes which will help you to create powerful applications and reduces the amount of Java code you have to write to a minimum. Since the API classes have been thoroughly tested you can use them with confidence to write error-free software fast.

The topics covered in this book include introductory material on the Java language itself, the use of the environment for creating and managing projects and also more advanced material on using the classes for file handling, creating and using graphics, developing Windows-like user interfaces and handling events.

One of the more controversial aspects of Visual J++ is that it includes the Windows Foundation Classes which allow you to create Windows applications in Java. This book covers the key aspects of the WFC and shows how you can create Windows applications as easily as using a Windows-specific IDE such as Visual Basic.

Learning a new language and development environment is difficult, and, like learning a spoken language, you have to have a lot of practice. It is recommended that you work on this book at your computer – checking that the screen pictures in the text match those on the monitor in front of you and trying the example programs for yourself.

What you need to run Visual J++

Visual J++ in common with all powerful IDEs requires a fairly well-specified computer. The typical configuration which companies like Microsoft and Borland expect professional developers to have is a Pentium II with at least 64Mb of memory and a 17" monitor; however, providing you are not running other applications at the same time I have found reasonable performance with the following specification:

- Pentium P100.

- 32Mb of memory.
- 15" monitor.

You can run Visual J++ with a poorer configuration, but it will be rather slow.

One problem with all IDEs is that they display a lot of information, so a 17" monitor or larger is a good idea, but you will not have serious problems with the standard 15" monitor.

You will also need a browser. MS Internet Explorer V4.0 was used throughout this book but you can use any recent browser which is Java aware. All the examples in this book were tested in a Windows 98 environment, but will work equally well with Windows 95.

What's new in version 6

Many programmers were disappointed with version 1.1 of Visual J++. Most of the problems with this version have been overcome with version 6 and in addition there are some unexpected improvements which combine to make this one of the most complete development environments available for Java. The key new features are:

- Inclusion of the Windows Foundation Classes (WFC), which makes it possible for you to develop Windows-based applications in Java.
- The WFC designer allows you to visually create Windows interfaces by dragging and dropping controls in a similar style to IDEs such as Visual Basic.
- The Application wizard helps you to produce Windows-based applications using the WFC.
- The Data Forms wizard helps you to produce applications which use relational databases.
- ActiveX Data Object (ADO) for the Windows Foundation Class is included so that you can write applications which use relational databases.
- IntelliSense helps you to type the right syntax for your Java code, for example by supplying a list of possible methods you can use for an object, and giving the parameter list of methods as you type.
- Improved debugging support, including multi-process debugging and remote debugging.
- Extensive HTML support, using a powerful HTML editor.
- Many methods have been deprecated, that is they are still supported but have been superseded.
- The event handling has been greatly changed to bring it in line with the Sun model found in Sun's Java Development Kit JDK 1.1 and later versions.

In addition the user interface has been greatly improved, making it easier to produce Java applications as fast as possible.

Conventions

This book uses the following conventions which make it easier to read:

- All program examples are in *italics*.
- File names and user defined identifiers are in *italics*.
- Java reserved words, classes and methods in the Java API are in **bold**.
- Class names always start with an uppercase letter.
- Method and variable names start with a lowercase letter.
- Menu options are in bold, for example, **File | New Project**.
- When a name is composed of more than one word the first letter of each word is a capital, for example, *ThisIsALongName*.

English spelling is used throughout, but the names of some of the classes in the Java API use American English spelling, such as the **Color** class.

2
The Visual J++ Environment

Introduction

The integrated development environment (IDE) of Visual J++ is shared with other Microsoft development tools, most notably Visual C++. Since many Java programmers have a C++ background it makes the transition to Java easier, however if you are new to both Java and the IDE you do have an extra overhead before you can begin to write applications or applets. If you are familiar with other development tools such as Visual Basic or Delphi you will see many similarities.

The aim of this chapter is to introduce you to the essentials of the IDE so that you can begin to develop your own applications and applets as soon as possible.

The Visual J++ environment

The Visual J++ environment is very flexible and can be configured in many ways depending both on the type of application or applet you are writing and also on your own preferences.

When you run Visual J++ you will see the New Project window which is shown in fig 2.1. At this point you must decide whether you are going to write an applet to run within a browser, an application to run within the virtual Java machine or a Windows application. Initially we are going to develop a Windows application. The aspects of the development environment that you will use will be different if you are creating a Windows application rather than a Console Application.

Choose the **Windows Application** from this menu. Fig 2.2 shows a typical user interface if you are developing a Microsoft Windows application. All of the windows can be moved, resized or closed, so your interface may be different to the one shown.

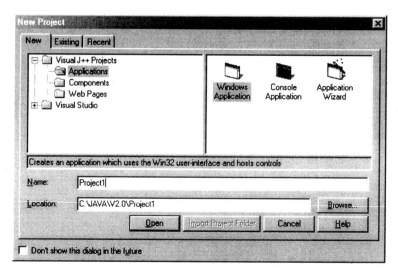

Fig 2.1 *The New Project window.*

If you are developing a console application which does not use Windows, some elements shown in fig 2.2 will not be applicable, and the simplified environment shown in fig 2.3 is more typical.

Properties window   Toolbox   Design window

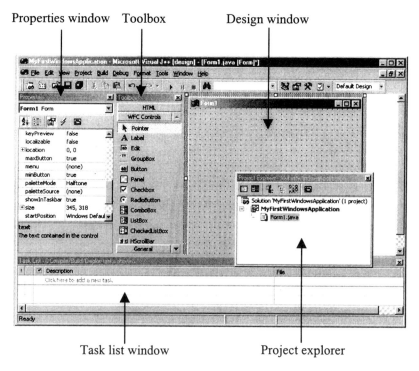

Task list window   Project explorer

Fig 2.2 *A typical user interface for developing Windows applications.*

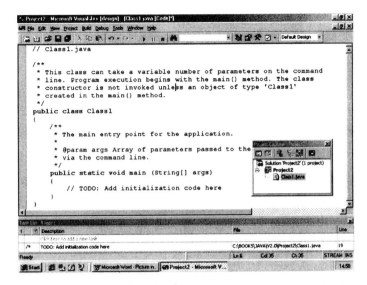

Fig 2.3 A typical user interface for developing console applications.

The missing Toolbox, Design window and Properties window are not needed to develop console applications.

The Project Explorer

If the Project Explorer is not visible in your environment select the **View | Project Explorer** menu option.

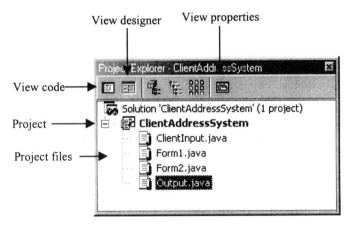

Fig 2.4 The Project Explorer.

When you are working on a large system it can be difficult to keep track of where all the files and classes are. The role of the Project Explorer is to display the elements of the projects that you want to see. To view a file double click on its name.

If you are developing a Windows application, a class may have a form associated with it. To view the code click on the **View code** button, use the **View designer** button to see the form as shown in fig 2.4. If you select the project and click on the **Properties** icon you are able to modify the project properties. Clicking on this icon when a class file is selected displays the Properties window, which is covered later in this chapter.

The centre three buttons display the elements of the project in different modes. The first of these displays the package view, the second the directory structure of the files in the project and the third shows all the files in the project.

The Task List window

If this window shown in fig 2.5 is not visible select the **View** | **Show Tasks** | **All** menu option.

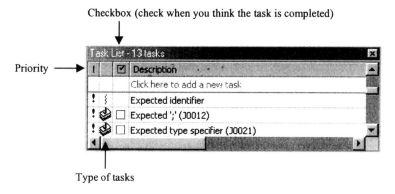

Checkbox (check when you think the task is completed)

Priority

Type of tasks

Fig 2.5 The Task List window.

This window has a wide range of functions. The most important is that as you type code, any errors are listed in this window and double clicking on a listed error takes you to the place in the code where the problem has been detected. When you build a project any errors are listed here and the message *Solution update failed* displayed in the status bar at the bottom of the screen. If you want more information on an error message displayed right click to show the speed menu and select the **Show Task Help** menu option. If the project builds without errors, the message *Solution update succeeded* is displayed.

A useful feature of this window is that the places where the comments **TODO**, **UNDONE** or **HACK** are listed. You can use the comments in your Java code to indicate that you need to revisit this area. You can move to the place in the code where this occurs by double clicking on that list item.

You can define shortcuts in the text editor by right clicking on a line of code and choosing the **Add Shortcut** option from the speed menu. A shortcut can be entered into the Task List window so that you can quickly move back it.

There are three levels of priority for the items listed:

- High is indicated by '!'.
- Normal has the priority field empty.

- Low is indicated by '↓'.

The type of item listed is given by the second column in this window:

   ¦   Indicates a syntax error found by SmartEditor.

   📚   A compiler error or warning.

   /*   A comment where **TODO**, **UNDONE** or **HACK** appears.

   🕯   A named shortcut in the code.

   📖   A user defined task.

The Toolbox, Design window and Properties window

The Toolbox(displaying WFC controls), Design window and the Properties window are only used when you are creating a Windows application.

To display these windows select the following menu items: **View | Toolbox, View | Designer** and **View | Code**. The design form and the supporting code will not usually be visible at the same time.

When you are designing a Windows application, the Toolbox, shown in fig 2.6, lists all of the Windows Foundation Class (WFC) controls that you can select and then place on the design form. The Toolbox also has a comprehensive set of tools for adding controls to HTML files, which can be displayed by clicking on the **HTML** button. An HTML file is needed to launch applets.

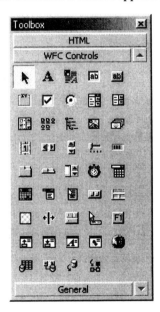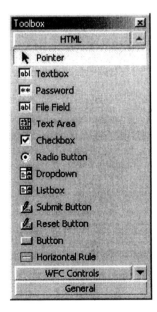

Fig 2.6 The WFC and HTML tools.

The Properties window shown in fig 2.7 displays the properties of the currently selected WFC or HTML control. The Design window, Properties window and the

Toolbox are central to the development of any Windows application and are covered in detail in chapters 14 and 15 on the Windows Foundation Classes.

Fig 2.7 The Properties window.

The standard toolbar

The standard toolbar is shown in fig 2.8. If it is not displayed choose the **View |
Toolbars** menu option and click on **Standard**.

Fig 2.8 The standard toolbar.

Everything that you can do with the toolbar can be done using the menu system, however it is good practice to use the toolbar wherever possible since it provides the quickest way of performing common functions. The toolbar functions can be broken into 5 groups, which are listed in tables 2.1 to 2.5.

Table 2.1 Project management icons on the standard toolbar.

Icon	Description
	New project. Displays the New Project window.
	Add Item. Adds items such as forms, classes and Web pages to the current project.
	Open Project. Displays the Open Project window to open an existing project.
	Save. Copies the current file to disk.
	Save All. Copies all of the files in the project to disk.

Table 2.2 *Editing text.*

Icon	Description
	Cut. Used in the text editor to cut selected text into the clipboard.
	Copy. Copies selected text into the clipboard.
	Paste. Inserts the text currently in the clipboard.
	Undo. Undoes the previous action. Clicking on the down arrows allows you to selectively undo previous actions.
	Redo. Allows you to do actions that you have previously undone.

The three most commonly used features of the debugger are included on the toolbar. If you want to display a more extensive set of icons for debugging choose the **View |
Toolbars | Debug** option to display the debug toolbar. Debugging is covered in chapter 18.

Table 2.3 *Starting and stopping programs.*

Icon	Description
	Start. Start executing the current project. If the project has not been built, or changed since it was last built this is done first.
	Break. Stops the currently executing program.
	End. Terminates the currently executing program.

Table 2.4 *Finding and replacing text.*

Icon	Description
	Find and Replace. Displays the Find window, which allows you to search for text and replaces it with specified text.
	Find. A drop down list of text you have previously searched for. Selecting an item from the list initiates the search.

One of the most annoying aspects of using a powerful IDE is that there are so many windows that it is not always easy to find the one you want. The tool bar has a set of icons displayed in table 2.5 which helps you to find these windows easily.

Table 2.5 *Finding windows in the IDE.*

Icon	Description
	Project Explorer. Displays this window.
	Properties Window. Displays this window.
	Toolbox. Displays the Toolbox.
	Task List. Displays this window.
Visual Basic	Load/Save Window UI. Allows you to save the current user interface you have set up, and also to use standard defined user interfaces or ones you have previously defined.

Customizing your environment

There are some useful features available in Visual J++ which allow you to customize the appearance of your environment.

- You can add a large range of toolbars by using the **View | Toolbars** menu option.
- You can move windows and toolbars on the screen to any position you wish. the **Windows | Dockable** menu option determines if windows can be docked or not.
- The Load/Save Window UI icon on the standard toolbar offers a range of user interfaces you can choose from.
- The **Tools | Customize Toolbox** menu option allows you to add new controls to the Toolbox.
- The **Tools | Options** menu option offers an extensive range of features which allow you to control every aspect of the user interface.

It is worthwhile experimenting to find a set-up which you prefer.

Moving on

This chapter has presented some of the key features of the Visual J++ environment that you need to know. At this point, the IDE should start to look more familiar to you, and most people are keen to start writing Java applications and applets. The best way to learn how to program is to get a lot of practice, this will also help you to appreciate some of the excellent features of the powerful Visual J++ IDE.

3

Creating Applications and Applets

Introduction

Visual J++ is a powerful IDE, but when you first start using it the complexity of the environment itself can cause you as many problems as the application or applet that you are writing. When you start a new Java project there is a sequence of operations that you will have to go through every time. This may vary slightly if you are using existing files rather than creating your own from scratch. In this chapter we are first going to look at the differences between applications and applets, next we are going to create both an application and an applet, so that later when you are learning some of the more difficult ideas of Java you will not have to worry so much about how to use the environment.

Applets and applications

If you use HTML to create a Web page, you can specify exactly the layout and content of that page and provide links to other pages. We take it for granted that you can view any Web page irrespective of the computer you are using or the computer used to host the page. All you need to view any HTML page is a browser such as Internet Explorer or Netscape. If you want to create an interactive page or to provide some animation the most flexible and widely used method is to use Java. Java programs which run within a browser environment are called applets.

Applications run on the host computer without using a browser. Until recently Java has been used almost exclusively for writing applets, but with the development of IDEs for Java, such as Visual J++ and Borland's JBuilder, Java has become an increasingly attractive language for writing applications, instead of using languages such as C++. This version of Visual J++ allows you to create Windows executable files which do not need a runtime interpreter. This significantly improves the speed of these applications.

There are some important differences between applets and applications because of the different environments they run in:

- Applets may not be able to access the local file system. This is an important security feature which prevents a virus written as a Java applet from completely destroying the files on your computer.
- Applets cannot communicate with the local server.
- Applets always have some sort of visual aspect.

In addition there are some differences between the structure of applications and applets which we will look at later in this chapter.

Creating an application

When you first start using Visual J++ you are likely to find as much difficulty coping with the environment as the language. In this section we are going to focus on the mechanics of how you create an application, so that when you try the more complicated examples later in this book you will not have difficulties with the procedures you need to follow to compile, link and run your application.

The application we are going to write is a console application and displays a text message on the screen.

- To start your application select the **File | New Project** menu option. Select the **New** page. The dialog shown in fig 3.1 is displayed. This dialog is automatically shown when you run Visual J++.

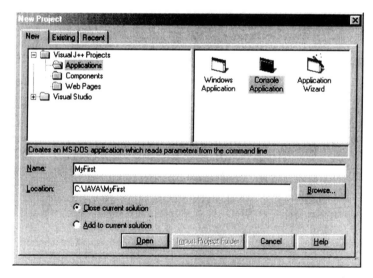

Fig 3.1 *Creating a new application.*

- Select the **Console Application** option.
- If you do not want to save your project in the specified **Location**, click on the **Browse** button on the right of this field to specify a new location.
- Type the name of your project, in the **Name** text field. In this case *MyFirst*.

- Click the **Open** button. If you already have a project open you will be asked if you want to save it.

This creates a folder with the same name as the project, in this case *MyFirst* for the project files. A class file is also created. To view this file double click on the name of the file, which will have a default name of *Class1.java*, as shown in fig 3.2.

Fig 3.2 The Project Explorer.

The default code produced by Visual J++ is shown below:

```
// Class1.java

/**
 * This class can take a variable number of parameters on the command
 * line. Program execution begins with the main( ) method. The class
 * constructor is not invoked unless an object of type 'Class1'
 * created in the main() method.
 */
public class Class1
{
    /**
     * The main entry point for the application.
     *
     * @param args Array of parameters passed to the application
     * via the command line.
     */
    public static void main (String[ ] args)
    {
        // TODO: Add initialization code here
    }
}
```

Most of this application is comment. In Java there are two ways of specifying comments.

- The characters // indicate that any following text on that line is comment.
- Multi-line comments start with the /* characters and end with the */ characters.

We are only going to add one line of code to this application which is to display a message. All Java applications start executing in the **main** method. Add one line to the **main** method as shown below:

> *public static void main (String[ ] args)*
> *{*
> *   System.out.println("My first application"); //display this text*
> *}*

As you type the IntelliSense facility offers you a list of possible options as shown in fig 3.3. To select one of the options offered you find the option you want and either double click on it or press the Tab key. It will be inserted automatically into your code. If you wish you can ignore these options and simply type the whole method name yourself. While this facility does not really speed up typing, it is invaluable if you cannot exactly remember the name or parameters of a method. This is a real problem in Java which has a very extensive set of class libraries including thousands of classes methods and variables.

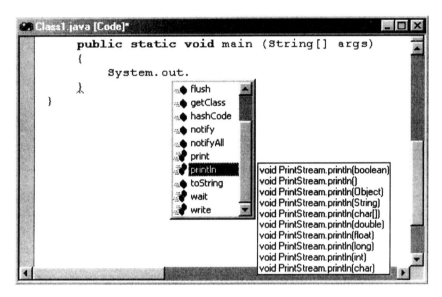

Fig 3.3 Typing Java code.

To build this application select the **Build | Build** menu option.

To run it select the **Debug | Start** option or choose the run icon from the standard toolbar. If you are unsure of which icon to use, move the cursor over the icons and a small pop-up message appears telling you what each icon does.

If you omit the build stage, Visual J++ detects this and will build the application before running it. If you amend the application and run it, it will automatically be built before executing.

The running application is shown in fig 3.4. This window will appear briefly and when the application finishes, after displaying the line of text, it will close.

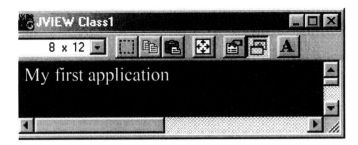

Fig 3.4 *The running application.*

When you run this application within the Visual J++ IDE the class file which is produced when you build the Java source file is executed.

Running the application outside the IDE

You can also run this application outside of the Visual J++ IDE.

- Go to the MS-DOS prompt, by choosing **Start | Programs | MS-DOS Prompt** from your desktop.
- Go to the folder which contains the application you have created by typing *CD your path name*.
- Type *JVIEW Class1*. Note that the name of the class is case sensitive.

If your computer cannot find JVIEW.exe, you may have to amend your path list to include the folder containing this file. It is usually installed in C:\WINDOWS if you are not using a networked computer.

Visual J++ also produces an MS-DOS executable called *MyFirst.exe*, which you can run by going to the MS-DOS prompt and then going to the folder containing the project as before. To run the application type the project name *MyFirst*. When running the MS-DOS executable the name is not case sensitive.

Creating an applet

We are now going to create an applet which will run within the browser. The process is similar to creating an application.

- Select **File | New project** option.
- Select the **New** page and click on **Web Pages**.
- Click on the **Applet on HTML** option, as shown in fig 3.5.
- Give the project a name of *MyFirstApplet*.
- Click on the **Open** button. You will be asked if you wish to save the currently open project.

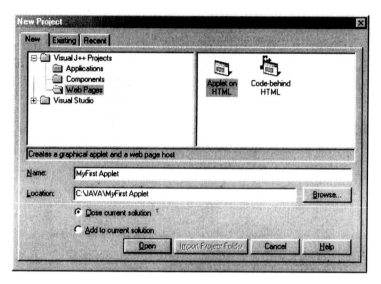

Fig 3.5   *Creating an applet.*

As for applications the Project Explorer is used to display the project files. Applets have at least one Java source file and at least one HTML file as shown in fig 3.6.

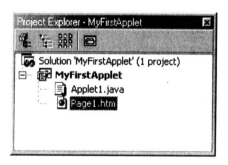

Fig 3.6   *The Project Explorer.*

To display the HTML file double click on its file name in the Project Explorer and choose the **Source** page. The HTML file created by Visual J++ is shown below:

```
<HTML>
<HEAD>
<META NAME="GENERATOR" Content="Microsoft Visual Studio 6.0">
</HEAD>
<BODY>
<P> </P>
<!-- Insert HTML here -->
    <APPLET code=Applet1.class codeBase =file://C:\JAVA\MyFirstApplet\
    height=131 name=Applet1 style="HEIGHT: 131px; LEFT: 0px; TOP: 0px;
    WIDTH: 294px" width=294 VIEWASTEXT>
    <PARAM NAME="foreground" VALUE="FFFFFF">
    <PARAM NAME="background" VALUE="008080">
    <PARAM NAME="label"
```

     VALUE="This string was passed from the HTML host.">\</APPLET>
\</BODY>
\</HTML>

If instead of the text after the *\<!-- Insert HTML here -->* comment you see a rectangle, you can show the underlying text by right clicking on it to display the speed menu and selecting the **Always View As Text** option. The display area for your applet can be changed by dragging the rectangle's hot spots or changing the height and width values in the HTML.

To execute an applet, you must start running an HTML file which has the **applet** tag, this specifies the name of the Java class file which is to be run, in this case *Applet1*. The **width** and **height** parameters specify the size of the area on the HTML page the applet will run within. The **param** tag specifies some information which is passed from the HTML file to the running Java applet. Three pieces of information are passed, a text message and two 24-bit values which are interpreted by the applet as a background and foreground colours. How colours are represented and used in Java is covered in chapter 16.

The Java code produced by Visual J++ is completely different for an applet compared to an application. Unlike applications which start executing the **main** method first, applets have no **main** method. The **init** method is run first which in the default applet calls two methods, *initForm* and *UsePageParams*, which initialize the applet, setting the default colours and reads the parameters passed by the HTML file. We are going to add a new method to this application. The **paint** method is called when the form is first drawn and also when it is moved and resized. The **drawString** method is used to display text. It has three parameters, the text to be displayed and the x and y co-ordinates of that text.

The **paint** method is shown below:

```
// Add this method to display the text "My first applet"
public void paint (Graphics g) {
        g.drawString("My first applet" , 50, 50);      // display this text
}
```

It should be inserted at the end of the Java source file, just before the final closing bracket.

The running application is shown in fig 3.7.

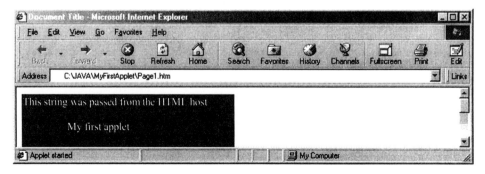

***Fig 3.7** The running applet.*

We look in detail at exactly what is happening in this method in following chapters, at this stage it is important to become familiar with the process by which you create and run applets and applications, so that later when you begin to write complex programs you will not have to worry about problems with using the IDE as well as coping with a new language.

Adding new files to a project

Visual J++ maintains a project file which lists all the names and locations of all the files which are used with that project. If you want to add a new or existing item to a project choose the **Project | Add Item** menu option as shown in fig 3.8.

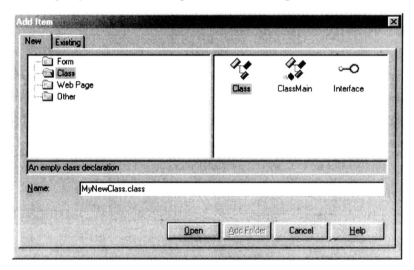

Fig 3.8 *Adding items to a project.*

You can add a new item, such as a class or form, in which case you must specify its name, or choose to add an existing item to your project. The item you have added will be listed in the Project Explorer and can be viewed and edited. When you rebuild all of your application or applet, the new item will automatically be included.

To remove an item from a project, close it, select it in the Project Explorer and choose the **Project | Remove from Project** menu option.

Copying projects

There is a common problem which often arises if you work on more than one computer. Since Visual J++ keeps a record of exactly where your files in your project are stored on disk if you copy the files to another computer which has a different directory structure (perhaps using Windows Explorer), you may find that your program no longer works. The error messages which Visual J++ gives in these circumstances are not helpful. If you do want to work on two computers, the best way is to ensure that both have the same directory structure. You may have to create a virtual drive on one computer, particularly if one computer you use is networked and the drive you use is called, for example E: and you only have a C: drive on the other computer. An alternative way is to use the **File** | **Save As** menu options in Visual J++ to save your files to a floppy or other removable disk and then repeat the process to transfer from this disk to your second computer. This can be tedious if you have a lot of files.

What comes next?

In this chapter we have looked at the process that you need to follow to create applications and applets. In chapters 14 and 15 we look at how you can create Windows applications and in chapter 20 at creating Windows-based applications which reference databases. The next stage is to look in detail at the Java language, which we are going to do in the next chapters. Since applets have the added complexity of HTML, we are going to use applications, which you will find easier to write than applets until you are more familiar with Java.

4
The Java Language

Introduction

Programs written in Java, in common with other programming languages, consist of data and instructions which use that data. For example, if you write a program which reads two numbers from the keyboard and multiplies them together, the numbers are the data and the operations which control the reading of the data and the multiplication are the program statements.

In Java, before you use a piece of data you have to state what type it is, for example if you wish to create a variable which represents the number of people in a room you would use a type which can represent whole numbers (you cannot have 2½ people in a room), that is, an integer type. If you want to save some text, such as a person's name you would need another data type, in this case a string type. You can carry out different operations on different types of data, for example you can multiply two integers, but multiplying two strings does not make sense.

There are some useful conventions which Java programmers tend to use when naming pieces of data. If you do not conform to them, your programs will work, but will look strange to other people. Since all substantial pieces of software are developed by teams, it makes life easier if everyone can agree on the same conventions.

As there are some additional complexities associated with writing applets, the examples are mainly applications, which are not run within the browser.

In this chapter we look at the conventions which Java programmers use, and how Java defines and uses data.

Java conventions

One feature of Java which often causes problems for programmers from other languages is that it is case sensitive, *FirstApplication* is different from *Firstapplication*. The examples in this book conform to the conventions which most Java developers use.

Class names start with a capital letter, for example:

class MyApplication

Everything else including methods and objects (we look at these later) is in lower case, for example:

int value;

If you use compound names which are made up of more than one word, the first letter of the second and subsequent words are capitalized, for example:

float longFloatName;

Java allows a fairly free layout, white space such as spaces and tabs are ignored by the compiler, as are comments. In common with C++ there are two ways of specifying comments:

/* If you want to have long comments which
go over more than one line it is easiest to use
slash star at the start and the star slash at the end */

// If you just want a single line of comment use two slashes.
value = count;   // this is a valid way of commenting a line

Java statements are terminated by a semicolon at the end of the statement. Forgetting to add a semicolon is a common source of error for new Java programmers.

Names in Java

In Java an identifier name is a sequence of Java letters and Java digits. There are a few important features of naming conventions in Java:

- The first character must be a Java letter.
- A name cannot be a Java keyword, a boolean literal (**true** or **false**) or a null literal (null).
- Names can be of unlimited length.

Java letters and digits are drawn from the Unicode character set which supports a large range of scripts available throughout the world, including Chinese and Japanese.

Java letters include upper and lower case ASCII letters A→Z and a→z, underscore and the dollar sign. They return a **true** value from the **Character**.**isJavaLetter** method.

Java digits include the ASCII values 0→9 and return a **true** value from the **Character**.**IsJavaLetterOrDigit** method, they return a **false** value from the **Character**.**isJavaLetter** method.

Primitive data types

Java is a strongly typed language, that is, before you can use a variable you have to define it by giving it a type. If you want, you can also give the variable a value at the same time. The primitive data types which are predefined by the Java language are shown in table 4.1.

Table 4.1 *The primitive Java data types.*

Type	Description	No. of bits
byte	Signed integer.	8
short	Signed integer.	16
int	Signed integer.	32
long	Signed integer.	64
float	Floating point.	32
double	Floating point.	64
char	Unsigned integer representing Unicode characters.	16
boolean	Boolean.	8

To declare a variable, specify the type followed by the variable, for example:

> ***int*** *count;*   *// declares a single integer variable*
> ***int*** *theStart = 10, theEnd;*   *// theStart = 10, theEnd is unassigned*
> ***boolean*** *yesNo;*   *// creates a boolean variable*

One noticeable omission if you have done some Java programming before is that **String** is not included in the list of primitive Java data types. This is because a string is not a primitive data type, but an instance of the **String** class, that is, an object. The clue to this is that the keyword **String** always starts with a capital letter, indicating that it is a class. You can, however, create and use **String** objects as if they were variables of one of the primitive data types.

Arrays

Arrays are lists of items. Each item in the list is of the same type, which is one of the primitive Java types. In Java, arrays are used differently to most third generation programming languages such as C and Pascal. Particularly if you are an experienced programmer the way in which Java treats arrays can cause problems. In Java arrays are objects.

To declare an array you specify the type of the array followed by its name, for example:

> ***int*** *values[ ];*

An alternative notation is:

> ***int[ ]*** *values;*

Just pick one of these and stick with it for consistency.

Next you have to create an array object. There are two ways of doing this. You can use **new**, which instantiates the array object:

> *values = **new int**[5];*

This creates a list of 5 integer items. The first is referred to as *values[0]* and the last as *value[4]*.

You can combine the two stages of type declaration and instantiation. The single line:

int[ ] values = **new int[5];**

is equivalent to :

int values[ ];
values = **new int[5];**

The array elements are initialized, 0 for numbers, **false** for booleans, null for strings and \0 for characters, however you can specify the initial values of the array elements:

int[ ] values = *{3, 45, 87, 23, 9};*

This defines a five element array of integers and assigns *value[0]* the number 3, *value[1]* the number 45 and so on.

When strings are initialized each string item is enclosed in quotes:

String[ ] languages = *{"Java", "C++", "Object Pascal"};*

If you want to change an array element you do so by specifying its name and the element that you want to change:

languages[2] = *"Visual Basic";*

A common problem in C++ is that if you define an array as having, for example, 10 elements and you try and write to an element greater than this at run time, unexpected problems can happen. It may cause the program to halt and give an error message or the program may continue, having overwritten a piece of data that happened to be at the place in the memory than you wrote to. This can cause chaos. Java has resolved this problem and checks to ensure that you only address array elements with the defined range. If you try and go outside of this range an exception occurs.

You can create multi-dimensional arrays, although strictly speaking this is really an array of arrays:

int table[ ][ ] = **new int** *[10][10];*

You address each element in a similar way, for example:

table[3][4] = *75;*

Arithmetic in Java

Java has the five usual arithmetic operators:

- + addition
- - subtraction
- * multiplication
- / division
- % modulus

The addition operator (+) adds two numbers together and can also be used to concatenate strings. The next application uses this operator. To create the project:

- Select the **File | New Project** menu option.
- Select the **New** page and choose the **Console Application** icon.
- Give this project a name of *TestingThePlusOperator*.
- Click on the **Open** button.
- If the Java source file you have just created is not displayed, double click on the name *Class1.java* in the Project Explorer.

Add the following Java code to this file.

```
class Class1 {
    public static void main(String args[ ]) {

        String firstString = "4", secondString = "7", thirdString;
        int firstInt = 4, secondInt = 7, thirdInt;

        thirdInt = firstInt + secondInt;        // add 4 and 7
        System.out.println(thirdInt);           // prints 11
        thirdString = firstString + secondString;// concatenate "4" and "7"
        System.out.println(thirdString);        // print the string "47"
        thirdString = firstString + secondInt;  //converts secondInt to a string
        System.out.println(thirdString);        //prints the string "47"
    }        // position the cursor here and choose Debug | Run to Cursor
}
```

As we saw in the previous application, when the application is run, the JView window will appear, display the results and close. If you want to examine the output in more detail, position the cursor on the closing brace of the **main** method (as shown in the Java code listed above). Choose the **Debug | Run to Cursor** menu option. When this line is reached your application will pause. The JView window will be minimized on the Windows 98 taskbar. To view it, click on its minimized icon. To finish the application, return to Visual J++ and choose the **Debug | Continue** menu option. The application will continue to run, and then terminate in an orderly way.

The output you will see from this application in the JView window is shown below:

```
11
47
47
```

When two integer values use this operator they are added to give the expected result of 11. The two string values are concatenated to give the string 47. What is less obvious is that when this operator is applied to a string and an integer value the result is 47, resulting from a concatenation. It is better to use the **&** operator when you want concatenation rather than addition.

The subtraction operator (-) subtracts one number from another.

The multiplication operator (*) multiplies two numbers together, the division operator (/) divides the first number by the second:

```
int number1 = 24;
int number2 = 2;
int result;
result = number1 * number2;      // result = 48
result = number1 / number2;      // result = 12
```

The modulus operator (%) divides two values and returns the remainder:

```
int number1 = 23;
int number2 = 4;
int result;
result = number1 % number2.      // result = 3
```

When 23 is divided by 4 the result is 5 and the remainder is 3. It is the remainder which is returned.

Assigning values

Java is a strongly typed language, you have to declare the type of a variable before using it. When you assign one variable to another, you use the = operator. If the variables are of the same type, there is no type mismatching, but what happens if you want to assign one variable to another of a different type?

In the following application, a **float** and an **int** type are multiplied to produce a **double** result:

```
class Casting {
    public static void main (String args[ ]) {
        int myInt = 3;
        float myFloat = (float)4.2;
        double myDouble = 5.7;
        myDouble = myInt * myFloat;
        System.out.println(myDouble);
    }
}
```

In this example *myInt* is converted to a **float** and multiplied with *myFloat* to give a **float** result. Since the result is assigned to a **double** variable, it is converted to **double**. The **float** type is stronger than the **int** type since it can represent a wider range of values, similarly the **double** type is stronger than the **float** type. Java supports implicit conversion from weaker to stronger types.

The statement:

```
myInt = myFloat * myDouble;
```

cannot be compiled and produces a compiler error, since Java cannot implicitly convert from the **float** and **double** types to the weaker **int** type.

The statement:

```
myFloat = 4.2;
```

also produces an error message, since the value 4.2 is implicitly **double**. If you want to convert a stronger type to a weaker type you need to do so explicitly. The following lines of Java compile and run:

```
myDouble = 5.7
myFloat = (float)4.2;
myInt = (int)myFloat * (int)myDouble;
System.out.println(myInt);
```

a value of 20 is produced.

Additional integer operators

In addition to the usual assignment operator (=) Java has a range of shortcuts available. If you want to assign more than one variable to the same value, you can use expressions like the one shown below:

```
a = b = c = 0;
```

All of the variables are assigned the value zero.

You can also combine the assignment operator with the four most commonly used arithmetic operators as shown in table 4.2.

Table 4.2 Integer operators.

Operation	Meaning
c += d	c = c + d
c -= d	c = c − d
c /= d	c = c / d
c *= d	c = c * d

Two of the most common arithmetic operations are to increase and decrease an integer value by 1. You can do this by using the ++ and -- operators. The following three lines of code all do the same:

```
myInt = myInt + 1;
myInt += 1;
myInt++;
```

You can also use:

```
++myInt;
```

which has exactly the same effect in this example, however this pre-increment operator does have a subtly different function to the post-increment operator as shown below:

```
int first = 1, second;
second = ++first;          // first = 2, second = 2
second = first++;          // first equals 3, two still second equals 2
```

The pre-increment operator increments the value of *first* from 1 to 2 and then performs the assignment. The post-increment operator carries out the assignment and then carries out the increment.

The -- decrement operator can be used in the same way as the ++ operator except that it decreases the value by 1. There are pre-decrement and post-decrement versions of this operator.

5
Java Classes

Introduction

Object orientation has become one of the most widely used and abused terms in program design in the past few years, some products which claim to be fully object-oriented in fact are not. Java, however, is a fully object-oriented language which supports the three key features of object-oriented systems: encapsulation, inheritance and polymorphism.

Java, in common with most object-oriented languages, uses a lot more jargon than a procedural language. Two of the most widely confused terms when programmers start to use Java are object and class.

In this chapter we are going to look at the distinction between classes and objects and the significance of encapsulation, inheritance and polymorphism.

Object orientation – a design approach

Many people who are not designing software systems are already using an object-oriented approach. It is widely used by hardware engineers. If the disk drive on your computer fails, the most likely solution to the problem is to buy a new drive and replace the one that has failed. It is unlikely that you will dismantle the drive to try and find the problem. The computer you are using is made up of a small number of components, such as a mother board, a processor, some memory, a graphics card, a disk drive and a monitor. Since each of these has a standard, defined interface you can connect components by different manufacturers together and expect them to work with each other. You do not need to worry about the internal construction of your memory, you just need to know that if fitted to the motherboard of your computer it will work as expected. This is an object-oriented approach. A complex computer can be produced by connecting a quite small number of objects together. Similarly if you are putting up some shelves you do not need to find a tree, chop it down and produce boards of wood before you can start, you just buy some shelving which has already been prepared. This approach seems rather obvious when applied to most of the manufactured items which we use today, but it is not the case for much software. One of the goals of an object-oriented approach to software design is to build software out of reusable objects each of which has a defined function and interface, so that it can be connected to other objects.

Most software which is not object oriented is custom made and a huge amount of effort is wasted writing slightly different programs. There are, for example, many word processors in the world and each of them uses a different spell checker, even though they all do virtually the same thing. If we had access to a library of existing Java classes which were fully tested, we could use them with confidence to build applications faster with fewer errors.

Classes and objects

When starting to use an object-oriented language, the terms class and object are often confused. A class is a description, or a template. We can, for example, have a class of bank accounts, which describes all of the information we need to store on bank accounts, such as the name and address of the account holder, the balance of the account and so on. A class will also have some methods, which are sets of Java instructions which carry out operations on this data, for example changing the name or address and displaying the balance. This class does not refer to any account in particular, it is just a description of what constitutes an account. A particular bank account is an object, sometimes called an instance of the bank account class. Similarly we can create a book class which describes the characteristics of books. This book is an object, that is, an instance of the book class.

In object-oriented programming we need to create classes, which consist of attributes or data, and methods or operations which perform actions on that data. To make use of the classes we create instances or objects.

There is over-use of the term object orientation, every software company wants to claim this of their products, but if you want to determine if a system is really object oriented you should see if it has the following three characteristics:

- Encapsulation.
- Inheritance.
- Polymorphism.

These are essential components of any object oriented system and are of crucial importance in objected oriented programming. We are going to look at each of these in turn.

Encapsulation

In object-oriented programming, data and methods are encapsulated into objects. The methods carry out operations or report on the data in the object. While objects can communicate with each other through defined interfaces an object does not know anything about the internal organization of other objects.

If you program using a graphical user interface (GUI), you will use objects such as buttons, forms and list boxes. Each of these objects has a set of properties (this is the data aspect of the object) such as the colour, height and position of the object. These objects also have a set of methods, which can perform operations on this data such as changing the object size or position.

Inheritance

Often when you are designing software you want use objects which are similar but not identical. If you produce each separately, a great deal of effort will be wasted. Imagine, for example, you are designing a GUI and have already created a simple button, which has a comprehensive set of properties and methods and you wanted to create some slightly different sorts of buttons. It would be very time consuming to start from scratch designing your new buttons simply because you wanted to support, for example, a graphic on the button face.

Inheritance allows a new object to inherit all of the data and methods of an existing object and to add additional ones. If at a later date you wish to create another variant, which perhaps has an animation on the button face, your new button can inherit all of the data and methods and add some new ones of its own. In object-oriented jargon child objects are derived from parent objects.

Polymorphism

One feature of inheritance is that all of the data and methods of the parent are inherited by the child, but sometimes you do not want this to occur. If we were creating an application which could draw basic shapes such as circles, rectangles, squares and triangles each could have the same attributes, for example, *fillColour*, *lineColour*, *xPosition*, and *yPosition*. Similarly each of these classes would have a set of methods, for example, *changeFillColour*, *changeLineColour*, *changeXPosition*, *changeYposition*, *calculateArea*, and *draw*. Each of these shapes could be defined as a class and have the hierarchy shown in fig 5.1.

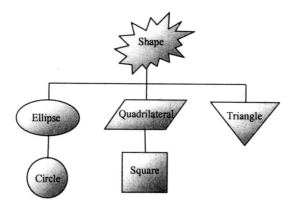

Fig 5.1 A shape hierarchy.

The *Shape* class is the superclass of the other subclasses. *Ellipse* is also a superclass of *Circle* as well as a subclass of *Shape*. *Circle* is a subclass of both *Ellipse* and *Shape*.

While some methods for these classes would be the same, for example the *changeFillColour* method, other methods would be different for each class, for example the *calculateArea* method. Polymorphism ensures that the correct *calculateArea* method is used. The *calculateArea* method of the *Circle* class overrides the *calculateArea* class for the *Ellipse* class.

Creating classes and objects

Most people read about encapsulation, inheritance and polymorphism and think that they sound like good ideas, but that they are no further on in the process of creating Java applications and applets. Usually these concepts only really make sense when you have looked at how you actually implement these ideas in Java and tried a few examples for yourself. In the next section we are going to look at a Java application which defines some classes and creates (or instantiates in object-oriented jargon) some objects.

The bank account hierarchy

The example we are going to look at is a class hierarchy with two different types of bank accounts. The two bank accounts are a savings account, which has interest added to it and a loan account which has details of the outstanding loan, and the monthly repayments. Both of these share attributes such as the name and address of the customer, but each has a number of different attributes to the other, for example the loan account has the initial size of the loan and the monthly repayments. The saving account has the annual interest rate applied to the balance. The class hierarchy shown in fig 5.2 is suitable.

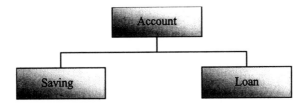

Fig 5.2 The Account hierarchy.

The *Account* class has the following attributes:

- Name of the customer.
- Address of the customer.
- Account number.

The *Saving* class inherits all of the attributes from the *Account* class and in addition has the following attributes:

- Account balance.
- Annual interest rate payable on the savings.

The *Loan* class, in common with the *Saving* class, has all of the attributes of the *Account* class and the following additional ones:

- Term of the loan.
- Number of repayments.
- Size of the loan.
- Outstanding balance, the amount left to pay.
- Size of the monthly repayments.

This has defined all of the data aspects of our class hierarchy. The next stage is to define the methods each class needs. The *Loan* and *Saving* classes will inherit all of the methods of the *Account* class and some additional ones of their own. The *Account* class has only one method:

- Display the name and address details.

The *Saving* class has this method and also methods which:

- Display the balance of account.
- Display all details of the account.
- Add annual interest to the balance of the account.

The *Loan* account has the following method:

- Display all details of the account. Note that this is different to the corresponding method in the *Saving* class.

This is by no means a complete analysis of the problem, but at this stage it is sufficiently detailed to illustrate how class hierarchies, encapsulation, inheritance and polymorphism are used.

Implementing the hierarchy in Java

After deciding on our classes, we need to do the actual implementation in Java.

- Create a new console application project, this creates a default class called *Class1.java*.
- Select this class in the Project Explorer and then delete it using the **Project | Remove from Project** option.
- Add the *Account* class to the project using the **Project | Add Class** option. Click on the **New** tab. Choose the **Class** option and select the **Class** icon. Specify a name of *Account*.
- Add the Java source files called *Saving* and *Loan* in the same way.
- At this stage, the Project Explorer page should look like the one shown in fig 5.3. To move between the files double click on the file you want to display.

First we are going to add the Java code for the *Account* class which is the parent class of the *Loan* and *Saving* classes. Open the file *Account.java* by double clicking on it in the Project Explorer. Type the following code for this class:

```
public class Account {
    String name;
    String address;
    int accountNumber;

    void displayNameAndAddress() {
        System.out.println(name);
        System.out.println(address);
    }
}
```

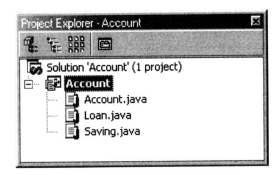

Fig 5.3 The Project Explorer.

Account is declared as the name of this class (in file *Account.java*) and followed by a declaration of the instance variables of the class.

The single method of this class is declared next. This method returns a **void** value and is called *displayNameAndAddress*. This method displays the name and address of the object.

Move to file *Saving.java* where we are going to define the *Saving* class. The Java code for doing this is shown below:

```
public class Saving extends Account{
double balance;
double interestRate;          // as a percentage

void displayBalance() {
    System.out.println("Saving balance is " + balance);
    }

void displayAccountDetails() {
    System.out.println("This is a saving account number " + accountNumber);
    displayNameAndAddress();
    System.out.println("Account balance is " + balance);
}

void addInterest() {
    balance += interestRate/100 * balance;
```

```
            }
      }
```

The first line:

public class *Saving* **extends** *Account {*

declares *Saving* as a class which has *Account* as a parent class. *Saving* therefore inherits all of the methods and attributes of that class. In addition the *displayBalance*, *displayAccountDetails* and *addInterest* methods are defined.

Double click on the *Loan.java* file in the **FileView** frame to move to that file. The *Loan* class is shown below:

```
public class Loan extends Account {
      int loanTerm;
      int numberOfRepayments;
      double loanSize;
      double balance;
      double monthlyRepayments;

      void displayAccountDetails( ) {
      System.out.println("This is a loan account number " + accountNumber);
      displayNameAndAddress( );
      System.out.println("Size of loan " + loanSize);
      System.out.println("Number of repayments " + numberOfRepayments);
      System.out.println("Outstanding balance " + balance);
      System.out.println("Monthly repayments " + monthlyRepayments);
      }
}
```

This class also has the *Account* class as a parent. It has a single method which is called *displayAccountDetails*. Note that there is a method of the same name in the *Saving* class which has a different function.

Instantiating objects – what's new?

So far we have defined our classes but not yet created (or instantiated in object-oriented jargon) any objects. There are two stages to instantiating an object:

Saving suesSavingAccount;
*suesSavingAccount = **new** Saving( );*

In the first statement *suesSavingAccount* is declared as a reference to a *Saving* object.
In the second statement the reference is assigned to a real object. These are usually combined into a single statement:

*Saving suesSavingAccount = **new** Saving( );*

suesSavingAccount is an object, that is an instance of the *Saving* class.
The **new** operator carries out two essential functions:

- Allocates memory for the object.
- Calls the constructor method for the object. This method is used to initialize the instance variables.

We look at constructors later in chapter 8.

Using variables and methods

If you want to use the instance variables you need to use dot notation, that is, you specify the name of the object followed by a dot and the instance variable, for example if you want to create an object called *johnsAccount* which is a member of the *Loan* class and that object has an instance variable called *name* that you want to assign you can do so as shown:

> *Loan johnsAccount = **new** Loan( );*
> *johnsAccount.name = "John Smith";*

You can use the instance variables in the same way as for locally declared variables, you just reference them a different way.

> *billsSavingAccount.balance = 99.2;*

The above statement uses the instance variable *balance* for the object which is called *billsSavingAccount.*

You can reference methods in the same way using the dot notation, by specifying the name of the object, the name of the method and then brackets:

> *billsSavingAccount.displayAccountDetails( );*

This statement calls the method *displayAccountDetails* for the object which is called *billsSavingAccount.* The brackets are used to enclose data which is passed to the method. If no data is passed the brackets are empty.

Using the classes

In our bank account application we have created all of the classes, the next stage is to create instances of the classes. We can do this in the **main** method which we can type below the *Account* class.

```
public static void main(String args[ ]) {
        Saving billsSavingAccount = new Saving( );
        billsSavingAccount.balance = 99.22;
        billsSavingAccount.name = "Bill Simmons";
        billsSavingAccount.address = "37 Maple Ave, NN3 3TL";
        billsSavingAccount.accountNumber = 5672876;
        billsSavingAccount.displayAccountDetails( );
        System.out.println( );
        Loan suesLoanAccount = new Loan( );
        suesLoanAccount.name = "Sue Collier";
```

```
        suesLoanAccount.address = "50 Weston Close, NG7 6GH";
        suesLoanAccount.accountNumber = 6986298;
        suesLoanAccount.loanSize = -12000;
        suesLoanAccount.numberOfRepayments = 60;
        suesLoanAccount.balance = -8644.32;
        suesLoanAccount.monthlyRepayments = 580.74;
        suesLoanAccount.displayAccountDetails();
        }
```

When you run this application it produces the result shown in fig 5.4:

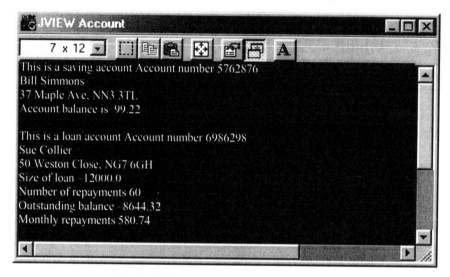

Fig 5.4 *The running Account application.*

In particular note the *displayAccountDetails* methods used by the *Saving* object and the *Loan* object are different.

Using methods

We have seen an example of how instance variables and methods are used, in this section we are going to look at this in more detail.

The *Rabbit* class can be used to calculate and display the number of rabbits based on their prodigious reproductive powers, this class has three instance variables:

- The *initalNumber* of rabbits.
- The number of *rabbitsPerLitter*.
- The *numberOfLittersPerYear*.

These are all integer values. There are two methods:

- The *howMany* method calculates the number of rabbits after a specified time period.

- The *displayHowMany* method displays that number of rabbits.

The instance variables are declared:

```
public class Rabbits {
    int initialNumber;
    int numberPerLitter;
    int littersPerYear;
```

To define the two methods, *howMany* and *displayHowMany* you must specify:

- The access modifiers - these are covered in chapter 9.
- The type of the object returned by the method.
- The method name.
- The arguments passed to the object.
- The main body of the method.

```
long howMany(int time) {
    int c;
    long number = initialNumber;
    for (c = 0; c < time * littersPerYear; c++ )
        number += number/2 * numberPerLitter;
    return number;
}
```

- In this method no modifiers are explicitly specified.
- A **long** value is returned, this type must be the same as that used in the return statement at the end of the method.
- The method name is *howMany*.
- A single argument called *time* of type **int** is passed to the method. This is a way of passing information to the method.
- The main body of the method carries out the calculations required and ends with the **return** statement which passes a **long** value back to the calling statement (since this method is declared as **long**).

The *howMany* method can be invoked as shown below:

```
Rabbits r = new Rabbits( );
long number;
int time = 5;
number = r.howMany(time);
```

In the *displayHowMany* method shown below, no value is returned, so it is **void** (and there is no corresponding **return** statement). Two arguments, one **int** and the other **long** are specified. It is necessary to use the **long** type for storing the number of rabbits since their reproductive powers are so great.

```
void displayHowMany(int time, long number) {
    System.out.println("In " + time +" years there will be "+ number + " rabbits");
}
```

Note that the names of the passed arguments do not have to be the same as that in the call to the method shown below, but they may be:

> *r.displayHowMany(theTime, number);*

The running application, shown in fig 5.5 produces some alarming output.

Fig 5.5 *How many rabbits in 20 years?*

The complete application is shown below:

```
public class Rabbits {
    int initialNumber;
    int numberPerLitter;
    int littersPerYear;

long howMany(int time) {
    int c;
    long number = initialNumber;
    for (c = 0; c < time * littersPerYear; c++ )
        number += number/2 * numberPerLitter;
    return number;
}

void displayHowMany(int time, long number) {
    System.out.println("In " + time + " years there will be "+ number + " rabbits");
}

    public static void main(String args[ ]) {
    int theTime = 20;
    long number;
    Rabbits r = new Rabbits( );
    r.initialNumber = 2;
    r.numberPerLitter = 4;
    r.littersPerYear = 1;
    number = r.howMany(theTime);
    r.displayHowMany(theTime, number);
    }
}
```

This application makes some assumptions: the rabbits live forever; none ever get killed; young rabbits are ready to breed at the same time as their parents. Fortunately these are not correct assumptions, if they were we would be in serious trouble.

Instance and class variables

Classes have associated variables which form part of the class definition, these are declared in the same way as local variables except that they are defined outside of a method, that is directly after the *class* statement, for example:

```
class ZooAnimals {
    String specie;
    String name;
```

This class has two instance variables. The class *BigCat*, shown below inherits these from *ZooAnimals* and has a further instance variable called *food*.

```
class BigCat extends ZooAnimals {
    String food = "Meat";
```

When a new instance of the *BigCat* class is created you need to specify the specie, the name and the food the animal likes to eat. In this case all big cats like to eat meat, so it is inefficient to assign the instance variable food every time. You do this by changing the instance variable to a class variable. This is declared in the same way except that the word **static** keyword precedes the variable declaration:

```
class BigCat extends ZooAnimals {
    static String food = "Meat";
```

Class variables are available throughout the class, rather than having a different variable for every instance. The result of this is that all of the instances of the class *BigCat* will have the variable *food* equal to the same value.

```
class ZooAnimals {
    String specie;
    String name;

public static void main(String args[ ]) {
    BigCat tiger = new BigCat( );
    tiger.specie = "Tiger";
    tiger.name = "Ben";
    tiger.displayDetails( );
    BigCat lion = new BigCat( );
    lion.specie = "Lion";
    lion.name = "Lulu";
    lion.displayDetails( );
    }
}
```

```
class BigCat extends ZooAnimals {
    static String food = "Meat";
    void displayDetails( ) {
        System.out.print(name + " is a " + specie);
        System.out.println(" and likes to eat " + food);
        }
}
```

In this application, food has been declared as a class variable and assigned the value *Meat*. This application above produces the output shown in fig 5.6.

Fig 5.6 *Using instance and class variables.*

Note that the statement:

tiger.food = "Antelope";

will also change the value of *lion.food*, since *food* is a class rather than an instance variable.

6
Making Decisions

Introduction

It is important in programming languages to be able to loop around some parts of the program or to take different actions dependent on the value of data. In this chapter we look at how you do this. If you know any procedural programming language, you will find the syntax of Java different, but the ideas will seem familiar. There are a few surprises in Java even if you are a C++ programmer.

If...else statements

In common with most programming languages the **if** statement provides a way for your programs to make decisions. The basic form of an **if**...**else** statement is:

> *if (condition) statement;*

The condition is evaluated to a boolean **true** or **false** value. If the condition is met, the statement is executed. In the example below, two **if** statements are used in the *okForJava* method to determine if enough memory is available for running Java (32Mb or more). If it is, the message *OK for Java* is displayed. The second **if** statement displays the message *Not enough memory for Java*.

```
class Computer {
    int memory;
    int monitorSize;
    int diskSize;
    String processor;
    int speed;

    void okForJava( ) {
        if (memory >= 32) System.out.println("OK for Java");
        if (memory < 32) System.out.println("Not enough memory for Java");
    }
```

```
public static void main(String args[ ]) {
    Computer myPc = new Computer( );
    myPc.memory = 16;
    myPc.okForJava( );
    }
}
```

This produces the message *Not enough memory for Java* since *myPc.memory* is only 16.

The *okForJava* method can be improved by using an **if**...**else** statement. This has the general form:

```
if (condition1) statement1;
else if (condition2) statement2;
else if (condition3) statement3;
else statement4;
```

If *condition1* is met, *statement1* is executed, if it is not then *condition2* is considered, if this is met *statement2* is executed, if it is not, then *condition3* is considered and so on. A maximum of one of the statements in the clause is actually executed. The new *okForJava* method now becomes:

```
void okForJava( ) {
    if (memory >= 32) System.out.println("OK for Java");
        else System.out.println("Not enough memory for Java");
}
```

You can have as many **else** clauses as you wish, for example, the *okForJava* method could be further extended:

```
void okForJava( ) {
    if (memory >= 64) System.out.println("Great for Java");
    else if (memory >= 32) System.out.println("OK for Java");
    else System.out.println("Not enough memory for Java");
}
```

More than two **else** clauses becomes confusing. Fortunately Java provides a better way of carrying multiple *else* statements using the **switch** and **case** statements as you will see later in this chapter.

You can have more than one test condition in **if**...**else** statements, for example:

```
if ((memory == 16) && (diskSize < 4))
    System.out.println(" Maybe you need a new PC");
```

The && operator means that if both of the conditions are met, the message is printed.

Comparison operators

We have not mentioned the comparison operators explicitly yet although we have used them. They are very similar to those found in other languages. They are used to compare expressions. The most common operators are shown in table 6.1:

Table 6.1 *The comparison operators*

Operator	Description
<	Less than.
<=	Less than or equal to.
>	Greater than.
>=	Greater than or equal to.
==	Equal to.
!=	Not equal to.

Note the difference between the assignment operator and the equality operator:

if (c == d) e = f;

This above line compares *c* and *d* and if they are equal, assigns the value of *f* to *e*. The following line of code has confused these two operators although at first glance it looks correct:

if (c = d) e == f;

This incorrect statement gives an error message in Visual J++ (unlike some other Java compilers which accept this as valid and produce unexpected results!).

Block statements

Wherever you can use a single statement in Java, you can use a block statement. This is a group of statements enclosed by a { } pair, for example:

```
if (memorySize <= 16 ) {
    System.out.println("Not enough memory for Java");
    System.out.println("You need at least 32Mb");
}
```

Block statements are very helpful when writing **if...else** statements:

```
if (memorySize <= 16) {
    System.out.println("Not enough memory for Java");
    System.out.println("You need at least 32Mb");
} else if (memorySize == 32) {
    System.out.println("You have just enough memory");
    System.out.println("48Mb would be better!");
}
```

```
else if (memorySize > 32)
    System.out.println("You have more than enough memory");
```

Switch statements

If...**else** statements can become confusing if you have more than a few **else** clauses. The **switch**...**case** statement provides a shorthand way of writing some **if**...**else** statements, although it does have its limitations.

The code below displays a different message depending on the value of the integer variable *cpuSpeed*:

```
if (cpuSpeed == 166) message = "Slow for Java";
else
    if (cpuSpeed == 200) message = "OK for Java";
else
    if (cpuSpeed == 266) message = "Good for Java";
else
    if (cpuSpeed == 333) message = "Great for Java";
System.out.println(message);
```

This can be neatly replaced by the following code:

```
switch(cpuSpeed) {
case 166 :
    message = "Slow for Java";
    break;
case 200 :
    message = "OK for Java";
    break;
case 266 :
    message = "Good for Java";
    break;
case 333 :
    message ="Great for Java";
    break;
}
System.out.println(message);
```

This does exactly the same as the **if**...**else** statements, but some people find it easier to read.

At the end of each **case** clause there is a **break** statement. The **break** statement jumps out of the **switch** construct. If it is omitted, the following **case** statements are also executed until either the end of the **switch** construct is reached or a **break** is found.

You can add a **default** clause after the last case statement, but before the closing *}* bracket. The statements following will be executed if none of the **case** conditions are met:

> **default** :
>   message = "CPU Speed not recognized";

There are a few limitations on the use of this statement:

- You can only test for equality, so you cannot, for example, test for a CPU speed <= 166.
- You can test for four primitive types, **byte, char, int** and **short**.
- You cannot use **float** or **String**.

Despite these limitations this is a useful statement that should be used in preference to multiple **if...else** statements wherever possible.

Looping constructs

Most of the programs we have looked at so far just execute the lines of Java code one after another – since your computer executes a few millions of Java per second you would have to write a lot of code for a program which took more than a second to execute. Most programs repeat the same set of operations again and again. Java has a set of looping constructs which allow the same block of code to be executed repeatedly with different data.

There are three types of loops in Java:

- **while** loops.
- **do...while** loops.
- **for** loops.

While loops

There are two parts to **while** loops. The body of the loop which is preceded by a condition. While the condition is met the body of the loop is executed, for example:

```
int c=0;
while (c <= 12) {
    System.out.println(c);
    c++;
}
```

This displays the numbers 0 to 12. The test condition at the start of the loop is evaluated and if it is true, the body of the loop is executed.

Do loops

These loops are similar to **while** loops and in most cases they can be substituted for each other. The code below performs in a similar way to the previous example:

```
int c = 0;
do {
    System.out.println(c);
    c++;
    } while (c < 13);
```

The body of the loop is preceded by **do** and an opening parenthesis. The **while** conditions follow the closing parenthesis at the end of the block.

In this example the code gives the same result, but this is not always the case. **Do** loops are always executed once, since the test condition is at the end. If, for example, the initial value of c was 13, the **do** loop would display the value 13 before ending; the **while** loop would display nothing.

For loops

One of the most common things that programmers want to do in a loop is to increment or decrement a value, **for** loops provide a way of doing this. The **for** loop has three components followed by the loop body. The general form of a **for** loop is:

```
for (initialize; test; operation)
```

For example:

```
for (c = 0; c < 13; c++) {
    System.out.println(c);
}
```

- Initialize, $c = 0$ in this example, initializes the loop, if you have a loop counter, such as c you can give it an initial value. Unlike C++ if you declare a variable in this part (for example, *int* $c = 0$), it exists only while the loop is being executed.
- Test, $c < 13$, is the test condition. The body of the loop enclosed in parentheses will execute while this condition is met.
- Operation, $c++$, is an expression that is evaluated every time the body of the loop executes. While this is usually used to increment or decrement a loop counter, other expressions, for example $c += 2$ could be used instead.

In the example above the parentheses enclosing the body of the loop could have been omitted, since if they are not found, the body of the loop is expected to be only one line long.

Quitting loops

Sometimes you do need to get out of a loop before it has finished, if for example an error occurs and there is no point in continuing. You can do this using the **break** and **continue** statements.

If the **continue** statement is used rather than **break**, the program will ignore the rest of the loop body, and go to the start of the loop again.

Most of the examples we have looked at in this chapter consist of code fragments rather than complete applications or applets. The application below displays prime numbers. It uses a **for** and **do** loop and the break statement.

```
public class Primes {
    public static void main (String args[ ]) {
//Display prime numbers either between start (=3) and limit (=19)
//or the first 10  - whichever occurs first.
    int start = 3, c = start, d, numberFound = 0, limit = 19;
    boolean prime;
        do {
            if (c >= limit) break;          //leave the do loop
            prime = true;
            for (d = start; d < c/2; d+=2)
                if (c % d == 0) {           //if a zero modulus it's not prime
                    prime = false;          //it's not prime so don't continue
                    break;
                }
            if (prime) {
                System.out.println(c);
                numberFound++;
            }
            c += 2;
        } while (numberFound < 10);
    }
}
```

If you have nested loops, **break** only exits the current loop, you need a break statement for every loop or to use labelled loops.

It does not matter how many nested loops there are or if they are of different types.

7
Java Operators

Introduction

Java offers an extensive range of operators – so far we have only looked at the most commonly used. In this chapter we are going to look at a much wider range of operators and their precedence. If you are an experienced programmer it is still worthwhile reading this chapter, since Java does have a few surprises even to a C++ programmer. In particular the way in which Java operates on strings is very different to C++.

Logical operators

Some operations result in a boolean value, that is either a **true** or **false** value, for example:

    If (c == limit) System.out.println("Limit reached");

The test for equality between *c* and *limit* gives a boolean value of **true** if they are equal and **false** if they are not. When a **true** value is found, the following statement is executed because the test condition has been met. Sometimes it is useful to combine tests like this:

    if ((c == limit) && (count != 100)) System.out.println("At limit, count not 100);

In this example, only if both *(c == limit)* and *(count != 100)* give boolean values of **true** is the message displayed. The left expression *(c == limit)* is evaluated first and if it is found to be **false**, the right expression *(count != 100)* is not evaluated.

Similarly the **or** operator || is used with a pair of expressions which yield boolean results, for example:

    if (c == limit) || (count == 100) System.out.println(At limit or c is 100");

If either *(c == limit)* or *(count == 100)* or both give boolean values of **true** the message is displayed.

If the exclusive or operator ^ is used in place of the inclusive or operator || it will carry out the assignment if either *(c == limit)* or *(count == 100)* gives a **true** value, but not if both give a **true** value. The full set of logical operators is given in table 7.1.

Table 7.1 *The logical operators.*

Operator	Meaning
&&	AND. Right side only evaluated if left side == **true**.
||	OR, inclusive or. Right side only evaluated if both left side conditions are **true**.
^	XOR, exclusive or. Right side only executed if either (but not both) conditions are **true**.
!	NOT. Used with a single expression. Right side executed if the condition evaluates to **true**.

The not operator ! is used with a single expression, if c is **false** !c is **true**. If the expression evaluates to **true** this operator changes it to **false**.

Bitwise operators

Unless you are developing low level applications it is unlikely that you will use the bitwise operators, if this is the case you can move to the section on operator precedence later in this chapter.

Computers store data as a sequence of bits, for example the decimal number 85 can be written in 8 bits as 01010101 as shown below.

128	64	32	16	8	4	2	1		
0	1	0	1	0	1	0	1	=	64+16+4+1=85

The bitwise operators work with the corresponding pairs of bits in two variables rather than on the values as a whole. Java offers all the bitwise operators from C++.

Table 7.2 *The bitwise operators.*

Operator	Meaning	Operator	Meaning
&	Bitwise AND.	<<=	Left shift assignment.
|	Bitwise OR.	>>=	Right shift assignment.
^	Bitwise XOR.	>>>=	Zero fill, right shift assignment.
<<	Left shift.	&=	AND assignment.
>>	Right shift.	|=	AND assignment.
>>>	Zero fill right shift.	^=	XOR assignment.
~	Bitwise complement.		

These operators are not commonly used, but they do reflect origins in C++ as a language which is able to deal with low level operations at the bit level.

These bitwise operations can be explained by using truth tables. For example the truth table for the bitwise operator & is:

Table 7.3 *The & operator.*

A	B	A & B
0	0	0
0	1	0
1	0	0
1	1	1

The & operator works on pairs of bits. Since a bit can either be 0 or 1 the truth table is able to show the output from the & operator for all the possible pairs of inputs. There are 4 possible pairs of inputs, 00, 01, 10 and 11 as shown in the first two columns, headed A and B. The third column in the table shows the output from these pairs of inputs. The & operator is applied to all pairs of corresponding bits in the variables concerned. For example 19 & 135. 19 in binary is 0000 0000 0001 0011. 135 in binary is 0000 0000 1000 0111.

$$
\begin{array}{ll}
0000\ 0000\ 0001\ 0011 & \\
\underline{0000\ 0000\ 1000\ 0111} & \underline{\&} \\
0000\ 0000\ 0000\ 0011 & 2+1 = 3
\end{array}
$$

The result of applying the & operator is 0000 0000 0000 0011 in binary which is 3 in decimal.

Similarly the truth table for the bitwise inclusive operator | is:

Table 7.4 *The | operator.*

A	B	A | B
0	0	0
0	1	1
1	0	1
1	1	1

19 | 135 is given by:

$$
\begin{array}{ll}
0000\ 0000\ 0001\ 0011 & \\
\underline{0000\ 0000\ 1000\ 0111} & \underline{|} \\
0000\ 0000\ 1001\ 0111 & 128+16+4+2+1=151
\end{array}
$$

The truth table for the bitwise exclusive or operator ^ is:

Table 7.5 *The ^ operator.*

A	B	A ^ B
0	0	0
0	1	1
1	0	1
1	1	0

19 ^ 135 is given by:

$$\begin{array}{l} 0000\ 0000\ 0001\ 0011 \\ \underline{0000\ 0000\ 1000\ 0111} \qquad \char`\^ \\ 0000\ 0000\ 1001\ 0100 \qquad 128{+}16{+}4{=}148 \end{array}$$

The shift operators move the whole pattern of bits either to the left or the right. For example, 18 in binary is 0000 0000 0001 0010. 18 >> 1 moves the bit pattern one place to the right to give 0000 0000 0000 1001 = 9.

18 << 3 moves the bit pattern three places to the left to give 0000 0000 1001 0000 = 144.

Shifting the bit pattern of a variable one place to the right has the same effect as dividing the variable by 2. Shifting two places to the right divides by 4, three places divides by 8 and so on.

Shifting the bit pattern to the left, multiplies the variable in the same way.

The assignment operators in this group simply provide a useful shorthand notation, for example:

value = value << 3

has the same effect as:

value <<= 3.

The bit pattern of *value* is shifted three places to the left, effectively a multiplication by 2^3 (=8).

Operator precedence

When a sequence of mathematical operations is carried out, the order in which this is done can be very important, for example:

c = 9 + 6 / 3;

If the addition is carried out first the expression becomes 15/3 = 5. If the division is done first, it becomes 9+2 = 11. In this case the division would be done first, since the division operator has a higher precedence than the addition operator. The operators, in order of precedence, are listed in table 7.6. If you are in doubt, or want to make it clear to another programmer who looks at your code later what the precedence is, it is a good idea to use parentheses, since operations in parentheses are always carried out first, for example:

average = (value1 + value2 + value3) / 3;

Table 7.6 *Operator precedence.*

Operator	Meaning
( ) [ ] .	Parentheses. The . operator accesses methods and variables.
++ -- ! ~	Increment, decrement, not, complement.
new	Creates a new instance of a class.
* / %	Multiplication, division, modulus.
+ -	Addition and subtraction.
<< >> >>>	left and right shift.
< > <= >=	Less than, greater than.
== !=	Equal to, not equal to.
&	Bitwise AND.
^	Bitwise XOR.
|	Bitwise OR.
&&	Logical AND.
||	Logical OR.
= += -= /= %= ^= &= |= <<= >>= >>>=	Assignments.

When operators have the same precedence, the leftmost one is carried out first.

Comparison operators all have the same precedence and are therefore evaluated on a left to right basis.

When expressions contain a mixture of arithmetic, comparison and logical operators, the mathematical operators are calculated first, comparison operators next and logical operators last.

Using strings in Java

The operators we have looked at are mainly concerned with mathematical or logical operators, but strings are very important data objects which we have not yet looked at in detail. Strings are handled differently compared to C++. In Java, strings are sequences of characters, and are instances of the class *String*, which has an associated set of methods that perform many of the standard string operations that you are likely to use, for concatenating or amending strings.

As we have seen implicitly, strings can be defined just as if they were one of the basic types such as **float**, for example:

String *channel = "Four", day = "Thursday";*
System.**out**.**println**(*"Babylon 5 is on channel "+ channel + " on "+ day);*

This code will print out the text *Babylon 5 is on channel Four on Thursday.*
An equivalent way of doing this is:

```
String myText;
String channel = "Four", day = "Thursday";
myText = "Babylon 5 is on channel ";
myText = myText + channel;
myText = myText + " on " + day;
System.out.println(myText);
```

You can even use the += operator and streamline the code further:

```
String channel = "Four", day = "Thursday", myText = "Babylon 5 is on channel ";
myText += channel + " on " + day;
System.out.println(myText);
```

Assigning characters, strings and boolean variables

To assign a single character, you enclose the character in single quotes:

```
myCharacter = 'a';
myNewlineCharacter = '\n';
```

If you want to specify certain non printing characters Java provides a special way of doing this as listed in table 7.7.

When assigning strings you can also use the codes for the non printable characters:

```
myString "Heading 1 \t Heading 2\n";
```

Table 7.7 *The non printing characters.*

Code	Description
\n	New line.
\t	Tab.
\b	Backspace.
\r	Carriage return.
\f	Formfeed.
\\	Backslash.
\'	' character.
\"	" character.
\ddd	Octal number.
\xdd	Hexadecimal number.
\udddd	Unicode character.

When you are using booleans you can assign them the values **true** and **false**, for example:

```
boolean learningJava = true;
```

Assigning objects

If you want to copy the variables assigned to one object to another you can do it using
the = operator, copying the values one at a time. Here is an example where there are
two instances of a class which describes computers and where the values assigned to
one instance are to be assigned to another.

```
public void class Computer {
    String processor;
    int memory;

    ....
    Computer myComputer = new Computer( );
    Computer yourComputer = new Computer( );

    .....
    myComputer.processor = yourComputer.processor;
    myComputer.memory = yourComputer.memory;

    .....
}
```

If you write *myComputer = yourComputer*, this is syntactically correct, however it
does more than just assign the instance variables, it actually makes *myComputer* and
yourComputer refer to the same object, so that when you subsequently change one of
the instance variables in *myComputer* or *yourComputer*, the corresponding instance
variable in the other is also changed.

Comparing objects

You can use the == and the != operators to test if two items are the same object, but this
is rather less useful than might be supposed at first. These operators do not test to see if
the same values have been assigned to the two operands. This can sometimes lead to
confusing results. In the example shown below, two strings, *one* and *two*, are given the
same text, which is displayed. Two tests are then made:

- To see if they are the same object, the == operator is used.
- To see if they contain the same text the **equals** method is used.

Since the two strings point to the same object they are considered the same object as
well as containing the same text as is shown by the outcome of the two tests.

If a new string object is now created which has the same text, but is a different object
to *one*, this is verified by the two tests. The running application is shown in fig 7.1.

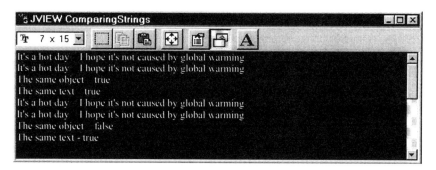

Fig 7.1 Comparing objects.

The code for this application is shown below:

```
public class ComparingStrings {
public static void main(String args[ ]) {
        String one = "It's a hot day - I hope it's not caused by global warming";
        String two = "It's a hot day - I hope it's not caused by global warming";
        System.out.println(one);
        System.out.println(two);
        System.out.println("The same object - " + (one == two));
        System.out.println("The same text - " + one.equals(two));
        two = new String(one);
        System.out.println(one);
        System.out.println(two);
        System.out.println("The same object - " + (one == two));
        System.out.println("The same text - " + one.equals(two));
        }
}
```

8

Constructors and Overloading

Introduction

We have looked at the essentials of how to create and use classes, but there are some important aspects that we have not yet looked at. This chapter looks at some powerful aspects which will form a part of virtually all serious Java applications. In particular we are going to look at:

- Constructors.
- Method overloading.
- Static methods.

Do not be put off reading this chapter because it sounds obscure and difficult! At first Java seems unnecessarily rich in jargon which makes it seem less accessible than other languages, but the ideas and concepts are worthwhile learning and will make it easier when you develop large applications.

Setting initial values

When you instantiate a Java object all of the class and instance variables will be assigned a default value, zero for numbers and false for booleans. If you want to have different initial values you have to do this explicitly. The obvious solution is to use the **init** method which is called when an object is created. The only problem with this solution is that there is a period in the object's life when it will not have the correct initial values and we have to rely on the application to behave correctly to initialise these values. There is a solution to this problem that does not depend on the application calling the **init** method.

Constructors

Constructors are methods that are automatically run whenever an object is created and are used to set the initial value of an object. Constructor methods have the same name as the class. Since names are case sensitive in Java, constructor methods will start with a capital letter (since by convention all Java classes start with a capital). All other methods should start with a lower case letter,

The *CarHire* class shown below is used by a car hire company for keeping a record of the servicing of its cards. Since the company always buys new cars and the first service mileage of new cars is usually 12,000 miles these values are assigned to the instance variables *mileage* and *nextService* in the constructor. The model and registration number will be different for each car, therefore these are assigned after instantiating the object in the *main* method.

```
public class CarHire {
String manufacturer;
String model;
String registration;
int mileage;
int nextService;

CarHire( ) {
    mileage = 0;
    nextService = 12000;
}

void nextServicing( ) {
    System.out.println("Reg. number: " + registration + " Model: " + model);
    if (nextService > mileage)
        System.out.println("Next service " + (nextService - mileage) + " miles");
    else System.out.println("Service is " + (mileage - nextService) + " overdue");
}

    public static void main( String args[ ]) {
    CarHire car1 = new CarHire( );
    car1.model = "Neon";
    car1.registration = "R238 LVF";
    car1.nextServicing( );
    }
}
```

The *nextServicing* method calculates when the next service is due. The application produces the output shown in fig 8.1.

You cannot call the constructor directly, it is automatically called whenever an object is created. If you do not supply your own constructor a default constructor is used which does nothing except initialize all non static variables.

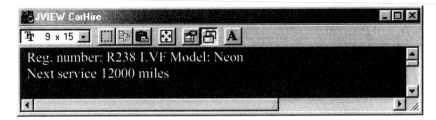

Fig 8.1 *Output of the CarHire application.*

Passing data to constructors

When you create a new object, there are some instance variables that you will want assigned to some initial values, for example if the first service mileage of a new car is always 12,000 miles the initial value of the *nextService* variable can be assigned this value in the constructor. If you want to assign initial values specific to the object being created, such as the registration number you can do this by passing arguments to the constructor. The **main** method is much simplified:

```
public static void main( String args[ ]) {
CarHire car1 = new CarHire("Neon", "R238 LVF", 0, 12000);
car1.nextServicing( );
}
```

In the constructor the arguments are read and assigned to the instance variables. The new constructor is shown below:

```
CarHire(String theModel, String theReg, int theMileage, int theNext) {
    model = theModel;
    registration = theReg;
    mileage = theMileage;
    nextService = theNext;
}
```

The output produced by this new application is exactly the same as that shown in fig 8.1.

Overloading methods

If you write a Java application which has two classes and each of the classes has a method of the same name this does not cause problems. If you refer to a method in a class, the method used belongs to that class. If, for example, you have two classes, *CarHire* and *BikeHire* and each has a method called *nextServicing* when you create instances of each called *car1* and *bike1*, each will use the correct method.

```
CarHire car1 = new CarHire( );
BikeHire bike1 = new BikeHire( );
```

```
car1.nextServicing( );
bike1.nextServicing( );
```

Java uses the fully qualified name of methods, which consists of the method name, the class name and the arguments passed to differentiate between methods.

You can also have methods which have the same name in a class, provided that they have different argument lists. This is useful if you have two methods which perform very similar functions and you want to give them the same name.

The first *nextServicing* method has no arguments and checks to see when a service is due, displaying an appropriate message.

```
void nextServicing( ) {
    System.out.println("Reg. number: " + registration + " Model: " + model);
    if (nextService > mileage)
        System.out.println("Next service " + (nextService - mileage) + " miles");
    else System.out.println("Service is " + (mileage - nextService) + " overdue");
}
```

If a vehicle has been serviced you need to change the value of *nextService*. The second *nextServicing* method does this.

```
void nextServicing(int miles) {
    nextService = miles;
}
```

This method has a single argument which changes the next service mileage to the specified value. The methods are called in slightly different ways, depending on the argument list:

```
car1.nextServicing( );          // when is next service due?
car1.nextServicing(20000);      //next service at 20000 miles
```

While you can have as many methods as you wish with the same name provided that they have different argument lists, Java cannot distinguish between methods on the basis of the return type.

If you have two or more methods with the same name this is called overloading.

Overloading constructors

Constructors behave like ordinary methods and so you could rightly guess that you can overload a constructor.

If you do not have full details of a vehicle, you could just rely on the default mileage of zero for a new car with an anticipated service interval of 12,000 miles:

```
CarHire( ) {
    mileage = 0;
    nextService = 12000;
}
```

The call to this constructor if you create on object called *car1*:

*CarHire car1 = **new** CarHire( );*

The *finalize* method

Constructor methods are created when an object is created, the **finalize** method is called when an object is destroyed, or at the end of the program whichever is the sooner. It is unlikely that you would wish to create your own **finalize** method except to optimize the garbage collection of an object, ensuring that all the resources such as memory which have been allocated to this object will be released. To create your own **finalize** method,

> **public void finalize( ) {**
>   ...
> **}**

This overrides the default method.

Using this

In the *CarHire* class we have created there are some unexplained things happening. Let us look more closely at a simple method, for example one of the *nextServicing* methods shown below:

> **void** *nextServicing(**int** miles) {*
>   *nextService = miles;*
> *}*

There is no explicit reference to which object the method is referring, so if you create two objects *car1* and *car2* and use the *nextServicing* method:

> *car1.nextServicing( );*
> *car2.nextServicing( );*

How does the method know which object is calling it? There is a hidden argument passed to the method, which is the name of the object. If you want to make an explicit reference from within the method you use **this**. The method shown below is functionally identical to the version shown above:

> **void** *nextServicing(**int** miles) {*
>   ***this**.nextService = miles;*
> *}*

If you do not include **this**, it is assumed that you are using the current object.

Class and instance variables

All of the classes we have created have a set of variables for each instance of the class, that is for every object you create. The registration number, for example, is unique to every object. These are called instance variables or object variables. Sometimes a variable will be the same for every object, perhaps the car hire company only rents cars made by one manufacturer. Variables which are shared by every object are called class variables or static variables. They are defined using the keyword **static**.

The definition of the instance and class variables for the *CarHire* class becomes:

```
public class CarHire {
    static String manufacturer;
    String model;
    String registration;
    int mileage;
    int nextService;
```

Note the keyword **static** before the definition of the manufacturer. Next we are going to add a new method which displays the model and the manufacturer:

```
void madeBy( ) {
    System.out.println("Model " + model + " made by " + manufacturer);
}
```

In the **main** method, we are creating two instances of the *CarHire* class. The class variable *manufacturer* is assigned the value *Ford*. This is assigned for every object of the *CarHire* class that currently exists or will be created.

```
public static void main( String args[ ]) {
    CarHire car1 = new CarHire("Neon", "R238 LVF", 12000, 10000);
    CarHire car2 = new CarHire("Puma", "R783 HUT", 12000, 10000);
    car1.manufacturer = "Ford";
    car1.madeBy( );
    car2.madeBy( );
}
```

The output shown in fig 8.2 shows that the *car2* object is made by *Ford* although *car2.manufacturer* has not been explicitly assigned to this value.

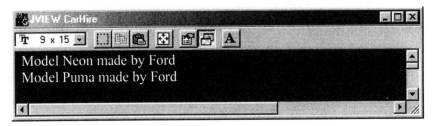

Fig 8.2 Using instance and class variables.

Static methods

Methods as well as variables can also be declared static, these do not apply to any particular object, but to all of them. If Honda were to take over Ford and we had to change the name of the manufacturer for every object we could use a static method:

```
static void changeManufacturer( ) {
    manufacturer = "Honda";
}
```

Note the keyword **static** at the start of the method definition. Since this is a static method, we cannot refer to instance variables, because we have not implicitly passed an object name to this method, however we can change static variables which apply to every object in a class. The *manufacturer* variable is a class variable (as it has the word **static** in its definition).

Calling these **static** methods is slightly different from calling non-static methods which refer to a particular object. To call a **static** method, precede the name of the method by the class name, in this case *CarHire.changeManufacturer*. The new **main** method is shown below:

```
public static void main( String args[ ]) {
    CarHire car1 = new CarHire("Neon", "R238 LVF", 12000, 10000);
    CarHire car2 = new CarHire("Puma", "R783 HUT", 12000, 10000);
    CarHire.changeManufacturer( );
    car1.madeBy( );
    car2.madeBy( );
}
```

This displays the worrying message that the Neon and Puma are made by Honda, shown in fig 8.3:

Fig 8.3 News of a worrying take-over.

Constant values

Some variables will not change for the life of the object. They are assigned a value when the object is created and remain the same. To do this you should put the keyword **final** at the start of the variable definition. In the *CarHire* class you might wish to add a final value which represents the maximum mileage that the cars will cover before being replaced:

```
public class CarHire {
        static String manufacturer;
        String model;
        String registration;
        int mileage;
        int nextService;
        final int maxMileage = 30000;
```

The integer *maxMileage* is assigned the value of 30,000 when a *CarHire* object is created and this value may not change. If you do try to do so, there will be a compiler error.

9

Inheritance and Polymorphism

Introduction

One of the key aspects of object-oriented programming is the ability to reuse code. Classes have defined class and instance variables and methods which the objects belonging to that class can use. If we can build up a library of reusable classes we can construct large complex applications and applets by combining these working, fully tested classes. Often when building your applications you will find that you have created a class which has some of the behaviour that you want but is not exactly what you need. Fortunately Java allows you to take an existing class and to extend it to form the class you want using inheritance.

We have already looked at inheritance and polymorphism, but these are such central ideas to the development of object-oriented software that we are going to take a more detailed look in this chapter.

Using inheritance

If you were creating an application for managing a library, you would want to create a class which retains information such as the name of the author, the title, the cost and the location. You would need some methods for managing the books, such as changing the location. If the book was a loan item, you would need some additional instance variables with the library number of the current borrower, the date it was borrowed, the return date and the loan period. If the book was only for reference, you would not need these items. By using inheritance it is possible for the *Loan* class to inherit the variables and methods from the *Reference* class as shown in fig 9.1. The *Reference* class is the superclass of the subclass *Loan*.

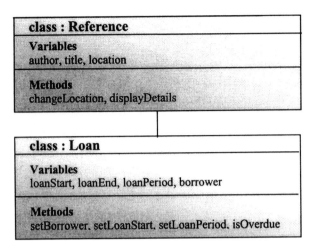

Fig 9.1 The Reference superclass.

In Java the definition of the *Reference* class would look like this:

```
public class Reference {
    String title;
    String author;
    String location;

    public Reference(String theTitle, String theAuthor, String theLocation) {
        title = theTitle;
        author = theAuthor;
        location = theLocation;
    }

    void changeLocation(String theLocation) {
        location = theLocation;
    }

    void displayDetails() {
        System.out.println("This is a reference item - not available for loan");
        System.out.println("Title : " + title);
        System.out.println("Author : " + author);
        System.out.println("Location : " + location);
    }

    public static void main(String args[ ]) {
        Reference r = new Reference("Oxford dictionary", "Oxford Press", "RE6G");
        r.changeLocation("BU7J");
        r.displayDetails( );
    }
}
```

When this application is run it produces the expected output shown in fig 9.2.

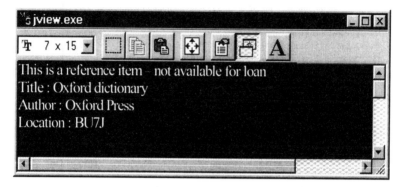

Fig 9.2 Using the Reference superclass.

If you want to use the *Loan* class you can inherit all of the methods and variables defined for the *Reference* class, by stating that *Reference* inherits from *Loan* using the **extends** keyword:

>   ***class*** Loan ***extends*** Reference

In addition, four new instance variables for the *Loan* class are defined, which deal specifically with the borrowing of books; these variables are not required by *Reference* objects.

>   **Calendar** *loanStart;*   *// the date the item is borrowed*
>   **Calendar** *loanEnd;*   *// the date the item is due back*
>   **int** *loanPeriod;*   *// the loan period*
>   **String** *borrower;*   *// the name of the borrower*

The *Loan* class has a constructor which sets up the instance variables to some initial values:

>   **public** *Loan(****String*** *theTitle,* ***String*** *theAuthor,*
>   ***String*** *theLocation,* ***String*** *theBorrower) {*
>   *title = theTitle;*
>   *author = theAuthor;*
>   *location = theLocation;*
>   *borrower = theBorrower;*
>   *}*

This class has several methods including *setBorrower*, *setLoanStart* and *setLoanPeriod*, the most interesting is the *isOverdue* method which checks to see if the current date is after the return date for the item. This method is passed a single piece of information: the date the item should be returned by. It displays the current date, the day the item is due back and a message indicating if it is overdue or not:

>   **void** *isOverdue(****Calendar*** *theEndDate) {*
>   ***GregorianCalendar*** *today =* ***new GregorianCalendar( );***
>   *today.****setTime(new Date( ));*** *//today has today's date*

```
System.out.print("Today's date is " + formatDate(today));
System.out.println(" due back on " + formatDate(loanEnd));
if (theEndDate.before(today))System.out.println("This item is overdue");
else System.out.println("This item is NOT overdue");
}
```

When an instance of the **GregorianCalendar** class is created it is automatically assigned the current date. To display the date stored in a **GregorianCalendar** object a private method called *formatDate* is called as shown below, which returns the date as a **String**:

```
private String formatDate(Calendar cal) {
    String[ ] month =  {"Jan", "Feb", "Mar", "Apr", "May", "June",
                        "Jul", "Aug", "Sep", "Oct", "Nov", "Dec"};
    String s = cal.get(Calendar.DATE) + "-";
        s += month[cal.get(Calendar.MONTH)] + "-";
        s += cal.get(Calendar.YEAR);
    return s;
}
```

The **before** method of the **GregorianCalendar** class checks to see if the date passed to it (the current date in this case) is before the date the item is due back, if it is, **true** is returned, if not **false**.

The *Loan* class method, *displayDetails*, overrides the method of the same name in the *Reference* class, that is, if a *Loan* object is created and uses the *displayDetails* method, it will use the method defined for the *Loan* class. This is called polymorphism. The complete listing for the *Loan* class is shown below:

```
import java.util.*;
public final class Loan extends Reference {
Calendar loanStart;
Calendar loanEnd;
int loanPeriod;
String borrower;
public Loan(String theTitle, String theAuthor,
                String theLocation, String theBorrower) {
    title = theTitle;
    author = theAuthor;
    location = theLocation;
    borrower = theBorrower;
}
void setBorrower(String theBorrower) {
    borrower = theBorrower;
}
void setLoanStart(Calendar theStartDate) {
    loanStart = theStartDate;
}
void setLoanPeriod(int theTime) {
    loanPeriod = theTime;
```

```
        }
    void isOverdue(Calendar theEndDate) {
        GregorianCalendar today = new GregorianCalendar( );
        today.setTime(new Date( )); //today has today's date
        System.out.print("Today's date is " + formatDate(today));
        System.out.println(" due back on " + formatDate(loanEnd));
        if (theEndDate.before(today))System.out.println("This item is overdue");
        else System.out.println("This item is NOT overdue");
    }
    void displayDetails( ) {
        System.out.println("This is a loan item");
        System.out.println("Title : " + title);
        System.out.println("Author : " + author);
        System.out.println("Location : " + location);
        System.out.print("On loan from " + formatDate(loanStart));
        System.out.println(" to " + formatDate(loanEnd));
        System.out.println("Borrowed by : " + borrower);
    }
    private String formatDate(Calendar cal) {
        String[ ] month =  {"Jan", "Feb", "Mar", "Apr", "May", "June",
                            "Jul", "Aug", "Sep", "Oct", "Nov", "Dec"};
        String s = cal.get(Calendar.DATE) + "-";
        s += month[cal.get(Calendar.MONTH)] + "-";
        s += cal.get(Calendar.YEAR);
        return s;
    }
}
```

To see how to use this class we can modify the **main** method to create an instance of the *Loan* class rather than the *Reference* class:

```
public static void main(String args[ ]) {
    Loan l = new Loan("Remains of the day","K. Ishiguro","HU7G", "SmithAJ");
    l.changeLocation("BU7J");
    l.loanStart = new GregorianCalendar(98,8,3);   //year, month, day
    l.loanEnd = new GregorianCalendar(98,8,24);  //months start at zero
    l.displayDetails( );
    l.isOverdue(l.loanEnd);
}
```

When the *Loan* object *l* is instantiated it uses the sole constructor defined for that class. The instance variables *loanStart* and *loanEnd* are given two dates representing the dates the item is borrowed and the date it is due for return.

The constructor used for the **GregorianCalendar** class takes 3 parameters, the year minus 1900, the month starting at zero and the day, for example:

*l.loanStart = **new GregorianCalendar(98, 8, 3);***

specifies a date of 3rd September (not August) 1998 .

The output produced by this application is shown in fig 9.3.

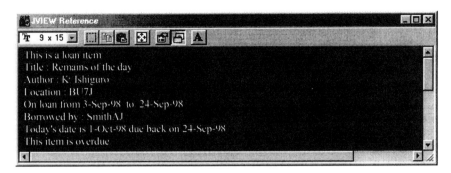

Fig 9.3 *Using the Loan subclass.*

Polymorphism

If we create a class hierarchy in which sub and superclasses have methods of the same name, Java decides which is the correct method to use. When an object uses a method, Java first checks to see if a method of the correct name and parameter list exists in that class, if it does not it looks in the superclass, and so on. This is known as polymorphism.

Abstract classes

You can create instances of both the *Loan* and *Reference* classes, but sometimes you may wish to create a superclass which cannot be instantiated, but its subclasses can. This is in fact a common situation where there is not enough functionality defined in the superclass for it to be meaningful to create an instance of it.

If we were creating a class hierarchy for a banking system, we may decide that there are three basic types of accounts, a cheque account, a loan account and a savings account. All of these accounts will share some common variables and methods, for example an account name, number and address and a method for changing the address.

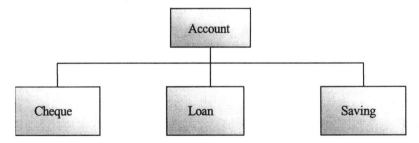

Fig 9.4 *The Account class.*

The *Account* class is called an abstract class since it does not contain enough functionality for an object of type *Account* to have any meaning. The purpose of this class is so that the attributes and methods which the three subclasses have in common can be shared rather than being duplicated in each class.

You can explicitly make a class abstract by adding this keyword in its class definition:

> **public abstract class** *Account {*
>
> ... ...

You can make a method abstract, which means that the method cannot be defined. An abstract method has no body. This sounds like a strange thing to do, why bother to define a method which does nothing? Abstract methods are used in interfaces which we look at later in this chapter.

Final methods and classes

If you want to ensure that a data member cannot be changed you can declare it to be **final**:

> **final int** *hoursInDay= 24;*

You can also make a class **final** which means that it cannot be extended, that is, it cannot have a subclasses:

> **public final class** *Loan {*

If you make a method **final** it cannot be overridden in a subclass.

Interfaces

An interface consists of a series of definitions of abstract methods – methods without a body, for example:

> **interface** *LibraryItem {*
> *displayDetails( );*
> *changeLocation( );*

If you want a class to inherit an interface, you use the **implements** keyword:

> **class** *Loan* **implements** *LibraryItem*

Any class which implements the *LibraryItem* interface must override the abstract methods *displayDetails* and *changeLocation*, therefore the interface ensures that the class must contain its own versions of these methods.

Java does not support multiple inheritance, that is, a class cannot inherit from two superclasses, but you can extend a class and implement an interface:

> **class** *Loan* **extends** *Reference* **implements** *LibraryItem*

Access control

One important feature of Java is that you can control the degree of access to classes, methods and variables. There are three access modifiers:

- **public**. Access is allowed by all methods in all packages.
- **protected**. Access is allowed by all methods in the class or in any subclasses.
- **private**. Access is allowed only by methods within the class itself.

In addition, if an access modifier is not explicitly given, access is called either "friendly" or "package", which gives access by subclasses and classes in the same package.

It is good practice to reduce the degree of access to the minimum, it cuts down on the number of possible interactions and makes it easier to spot errors when they do occur.

A class called *ClassOne* contains methods with each of the four possible access controllers. Table 9.1 shows whether each of the four methods can be accessed by other methods in:

- *ClassOne* itself.
- *ClassTwo* which is a subclass of *ClassOne*.
- *ClassThree* which is not a subclass of *ClassOne* but is in the same package.
- *ClassFour* which is not a subclass of *ClassOne* and is not in the same package.

Table 9.1 *Access controllers.*

	ClassOne	ClassTwo	ClassThree	ClassFour
public	✓	✓	✓	✓
"friendly"	✓	✓	✓	✗
protected	✓	✓	✗	✗
private	✓	✗	✗	✗

For example, the protected method in *ClassOne* can be accessed by other methods in *ClassOne* and *ClassTwo*, but not by *ClassThree* and *ClassFour*.

The access controller precedes the name of the method when it is defined.

10
Event Handling

Introduction

In a Windows system, events are occurring all the time. Every time you press a key or move the mouse several events occur. Java provides the capability to handle events so that you can take some specific action depending on which event has happened. In this chapter we are going to look at the mouse and keyboard events. In the next chapter we will be using the Abstract Windowing Toolkit (AWT) packages to create graphical interfaces and handling the events associated with these graphical components.

This version of Visual J++ supports an updated version of event handling, first introduced in Sun's JDK1.1 attaches a specific listener to objects that produce events in which you are interested. The previous model is still supported but is now deprecated, so there is no guarantee that it will continue to be supported indefinitely. It is strongly advised that you do not attempt to mix the two models, the possible results are described in Sun's documentation as unpredictable.

If you have used the previous model your applications will still work, but you will receive a warning telling you that the methods and classes you have used have been deprecated.

The MouseListener interface

There are two listener interfaces for receiving mouse events, one for events relating to mouse motion, **MouseMotionListener,** and the other for all other mouse events, which is called **MouseListener**. Both are in the **java.awt.event** package, and both receive mouse events which occur on a component.

The **MouseListener** interface has five methods, which each receive different events, listed in table 10.1.

Since Java does not support multiple inheritance you cannot extend more than one class, therefore if for example you are creating an applet which extends the **Applet** class you cannot also extend a second class, but you can implement the **MouseListener** interface. The real problem with implementing an interface is that you must implement all of the methods in the interface. If you only wish to use one of them, the others will be empty.

Table 10.1 *Methods of the **MouseListener** interface.*

Method	Circumstance causing method to be invoked
mouseClicked(MouseEvent)	The mouse is clicked on a component.
mouseEntered(MouseEvent)	The mouse enters a component.
mouseExited(MouseEvent)	The mouse leaves a component.
mousePressed(MouseEvent)	A mouse button is pressed.
mouseReleased(MouseEvent)	A mouse button is released.

The **MouseAdapter** class has methods of the same name as the **MouseListener** interface. It is an abstract class which implements the **MouseListener** class. All of its methods are empty. This class can be used in situations where you can extend it and override the methods which you wish to use. The advantage is that you do not need to include all of the methods defined for the **MouseAdapter** class. You will see how to use both the **MouseAdapter** class and the **MouseListener** interface later in this chapter.

The applet we are going to create displays the name of the mouse event, the mouse co-ordinates and changes the colour of the applet panel. The running applet is shown in fig 10.1.

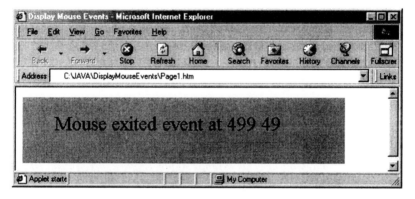

Fig 10.1 Displaying mouse events and co-ordinates.

In addition to the **java.applet.*** and **java.awt.*** packages, the **java.awt.event.*** package must be imported. Since we are developing an applet which extends the **Applet** class we cannot extend the **MouseAdapter** class as well, therefore we must implement the **MouseListener** interface:

> *public class DisplayMouseEvents **extends Applet implements MouseListener** {*
>   *String message;*

In the constructor for this class there is only one line of code:

> *public DisplayMouseEvents( ) {*
>   *addMouseListener(this);*
> *}*

This makes the applet panel a listener for the mouse events. When a mouse event occurs the appropriate method is called, for example when a mouse button is pressed the **mousePressed** method is called:

```
public void mousePressed(MouseEvent e) {
    display("Mouse pressed event", e.getX(),e.getY(),Color.cyan);
}
```

The **mousePressed** method in common with all of the methods of this interface is passed a **MouseEvent** object. A **private** method called *display* is called. It is passed four parameters:

- A string which identifies the event which has occurred.
- The x and y co-ordinates of the position where the event occurred. These are found using the **getX** and **getY** methods of the **MouseEvent** class.
- A colour.

The *display* method displays the text string it has been passed and the co-ordinates. It also changes the colour of the applet panel:

```
private void display(String evt, int x, int y, Color c) {
    message = evt + " at " + x + " " + y;
    setBackground(c);
    repaint();
}
```

The completed application is shown below.

```
import java.applet.*;
import java.awt.*;
import java.awt.event.*;

public class DisplayMouseEvents extends Applet implements MouseListener {
    String message;
    public DisplayMouseEvents() {
        addMouseListener(this);
    }

    public void mouseClicked(MouseEvent e) {
        display("Mouse clicked event", e.getX(),e.getY(),Color.orange);
    }
    public void mousePressed(MouseEvent e) {
        display("Mouse pressed event", e.getX(),e.getY(),Color.cyan);
    }
    public void mouseReleased(MouseEvent e) {
        display("Mouse released event", e.getX(),e.getY(),Color.pink);
    }
    public void mouseEntered(MouseEvent e) {
        display("Mouse entered event", e.getX(), e.getY(), Color.blue);
    }
```

```
public void mouseExited(MouseEvent e) {
    display("Mouse exited event", e.getX( ), e.getY( ), Color.green);
}

private void display(String evt, int x, int y, Color c) {
    message = evt + " at " + x + " " + y;
    setBackground(c);
    repaint( );
}
public void paint(Graphics g) {
    g.setFont(new Font("TimesRoman", Font.PLAIN, 30));
    g.drawString(message, 50, 50);
}
}
```

The Scribbling applet

The Scribbling applet tracks the movement of the mouse when it is dragged, the running applet is shown in fig 10.2.

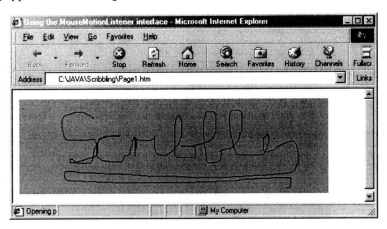

Fig 10.2 The Scribbling applet.

There are two methods in the **MouseMotionListener** interface which receive the two remaining mouse events not received by the **MouseListener** interface, these are shown in table 10.2:

Table 10.2 Methods of the MouseMotionListener interface.

Method	Circumstance causing method to be invoked
mouseDragged(MouseEvent)	The mouse is dragged, that is moved with a button pressed.
mouseMoved(MouseEvent)	The mouse is moved.

In the **paint** method of this applet, the **drawLine** method is used to draw the line between the position where the last mouse drag event occurred and the current position. This method requires the start and end co-ordinates of the line which is to be drawn. These co-ordinates are stored in two instance variables called *start* and *finish* which are members of the **Point** class.   Objects of this class have two instance variables for representing x and y co-ordinates. The x and y co-ordinates of start are given by *start.x* and *start.y*.

In the **mouseDragged** method shown below, a **MouseEvent** object is passed to the method:

```
public void mouseDragged(MouseEvent evt) {
    start = finish;
    finish = new Point(evt.getX( ), evt.getY( ));
    if (!first) repaint( );
    first = false;
}
```

The start position of the line is the finish position of the previous line drawn, this ensures that the line is continuous. The finish position is assigned to the current x and y position. The **repaint** method is called to draw the new line. The **repaint** method calls the **update** method which clears the drawing area of the applet and then calls the **repaint** method. Since we do not want the lines we have already to be erased every time a new line is added we have to override the **update** method with our own, which simply calls the **repaint** method.

Since the first time a mouse drag event occurs there is no start position the **paint** method is not called if the boolean instance variable *first* is **true**.

The completed applet is shown below:

```
import java.awt. *;
import java.awt.event. *;
public class Applet1 extends java.applet.Applet implements MouseMotionListener{
    Point start;
    Point finish;
    boolean first = true;

    public Applet1( ) {
        setBackground(Color.green);
        addMouseMotionListener(this);
    }

    public void mouseDragged(MouseEvent evt) {
        start = finish;
        finish = new Point(evt.getX( ), evt.getY( ));
        if (!first) repaint( );
        first = false;
    }

    public void mouseMoved(MouseEvent evt) {
    }
```

```
public void update(Graphics g) {
    paint(g);
}

public void paint(Graphics g) {
    g.drawLine(start.x, start.y, finish.x, finish.y);
}
}
```

In this applet we have implemented the **MouseMotionListener** interface, since we must override all of the methods of an interface we need an empty **mouseMoved** method. There is an alternative technique which could be used where an inner class is created which extends the **MouseMotionAdapter** class. When a class is extended (as opposed to implementing an interface) it is not necessary to override all the methods, and an empty **mouseMoved** method is not required. The applet listed below does exactly the same as the previous applet, but uses an inner class:

```
import java.awt.*;
import java.awt.event.*;
public class Applet1 extends java.applet.Applet {
    Point start;
    Point finish;
    boolean first = true;

    private final class MyListener extends MouseMotionAdapter {
        public void mouseDragged(MouseEvent evt) {
            start = finish;
            finish = new Point(evt.getX( ),evt.getY( ));
            if (!first) repaint( );
            first = false;
        }
    }

    public Applet1( ) {
        setBackground(Color.green);
        MyListener m = new MyListener( );
        addMouseMotionListener(m);
    }
    public void update(Graphics g) {
        paint(g);
    }

    public void paint(Graphics g) {
            g.drawLine(start.x, start.y, finish.x, finish.y);
    }
}
```

The key differences between the two applets is that in the second:

- The class does not implement the **MouseMotionListener** interface.
- The *Applet1* class contains an inner class called *MyListener* which extends the **MouseMotionAdapter** class.
- The **mouseDragged** method is in the inner class in the second applet.
- There is no empty **mouseMoved** method.
- In the constructor for the *Applet1* class, an instance of the inner class is created and is registered as a listener.

Generally it is better to extend the appropriate adapter class in situations where you do not wish to deal with all of the events which the listener will detect. This avoids the need to create empty methods which you will have to do if you implement the listener interface. An adapter class and its listener interface have methods of the same name.

The KeyAdaptor class

If you want to detect and use the events which occur when a key is pressed, you need to use the **KeyAdaptor** class or the corresponding **KeyListener** interface.

The **KeyAdapter** class has three methods **keyPressed, keyReleased** and **keyTyped** for handling keyboard events. A **keyTyped** event is produced by a **keyPressed** event followed by a **keyReleased** event. All three of these methods are passed a **KeyEvent** object.

The **KeyEvent** class has some integer class constants representing the key pressed, the most commonly used ones are shown in table 10.3.

Table 10.3 KeyEvent class constants for special purpose keys.

Constant	Key represented
VK_DOWN	Down arrow.
VK_HOME	Home key (start of line).
VK_LEFT	Left arrow key.
VK_PAGE_DOWN	Page down.
VK_PAGE_UP	Page up.
VK_RIGHT	Right arrow key.
VK_UP	Up arrow.
VK_F1 → **VK_F12**	One of the twelve function keys.
VK_UNDEFINED	No defined key has been pressed.
VK_0 → **VK_9**	One of the numeric characters.
VK_A → **VK_Z**	One of the letters.

There are many of these virtual key codes representing most of the keyboard characters. These codes represent which key has been pressed, not the character resulting from pressing a combination of keys, for example Shift+a will cause a **KEY_PRESSED** event with a **VK_SHIFT** key code, followed by a **VK_A** key code. When the 'a' key is released a **KEY_RELEASED** event occurs with a **VK_A** key code and finally a **KEY_TYPED** event with a key character value of 'A'.

These virtual key codes should be used with caution. Not all keyboards are capable of producing all these codes, and Sun have issued a warning that all of these key codes apart from those defined by the Java language (**VK_ENTER, VK_BACK_SPACE** and **VK_TAB**) may change in the future to cope with new keyboards.

The **KeyEvent** class has a set of methods which allow you to find the key pressed and to modify it if required, as shown in table 10.4:

Table 10.4 *Methods of the **KeyEvent** class.*

Method	Description
getKeyChar( )	Returns the character associated with this event.
getKeyCode( )	Returns the integer key code associated with this event.
setKeyCode(int)	Changes the integer key code.
setKeyChar(char)	Changes the character associated with this event.
getKeyChar( )	Returns the character associated with this event.
getKeyText( )	Returns a string which describes the key code, for example "HOME" or "2".

The DrawingLines applet

In this applet we are going to see how to use the **KeyAdapter** class and to take a different action depending on which key has been pressed.

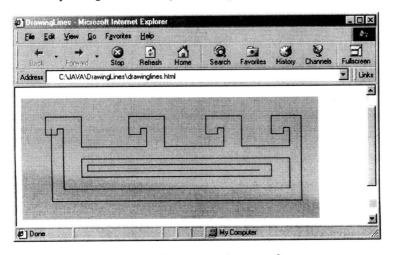

Fig 10.3 The DrawingLines applet.

In the running applet shown in fig 10.3, whenever one of the arrowed keys is pressed a line is drawn in that direction.

This is similar to the Scribbling applet; two **Point** objects *start* and *finish* are defined as instance variables of the *DrawingLines* applet, these are instantiated in the constructor method and both given co-ordinates of 50,50.

An instance of the *MyListener* class is created. This class extends the **KeyAdapter** class. It has only one method, **keyPressed**, which is called whenever a key is pressed. This method is passed a **KeyEvent** object. The **getKeyCode** method of the **KeyEvent** class is used to determine what this key was. If it is one of the arrowed keys the *draw* method is called with different parameter values for each of the four keys.

```
public final class MyListener extends KeyAdapter {
    public void keyPressed(KeyEvent e) {
        switch(e.getKeyCode()) {    // switch depending on key pressed
            case KeyEvent.VK_UP :       draw(0,-10);
                                        break;
            case KeyEvent.VK_DOWN : draw(0,10);
                                        break;
            case KeyEvent.VK_LEFT :   draw(-10,0);
                                        break;
            case KeyEvent.VK_RIGHT :draw(10,0);
        }
    }
```

The *draw* method calls the **setLocation** method (which replaces the deprecated **move** method) of the **Point** objects *start* and *finish* to change the x and y co-ordinates they represent, in this case by adding the values passed to the *draw* method. Finally the *draw* method calls the **repaint** method which draws the new line as shown below:

```
void draw(int dx, int dy) {
    start.setLocation(finish.x, finish.y);
    finish.setLocation(start.x + dx, start.y + dy);
    repaint();
    }
} // end of the MyListener class
```

This applet overrides the **update** method with its own which simply calls **paint** and so does not erase the drawing area every time **paint** is called.

The complete applet is shown below:

```
import java.applet.*;
import java.awt.*;
import java.awt.event.*;

public class DrawingLines extends Applet
{
Point start;
Point finish;

    public DrawingLines()
    {
    setBackground(Color.cyan);
        //start at co-ordinates 50, 50
        start = new Point(50, 50);
        finish = new Point(50, 50);
```

```
            MyListener m = new MyListener( );
            addKeyListener(m);
    }

    public final class MyListener extends KeyAdapter {
        public void keyPressed(KeyEvent e) {
            switch(e.getKeyCode( )) {    // switch depending on key pressed
                case KeyEvent.VK_UP :      draw(0,-10);
                                           break;
                case KeyEvent.VK_DOWN : draw(0,10);
                                           break;
                case KeyEvent.VK_LEFT :   draw(-10,0);
                                           break;
                case KeyEvent.VK_RIGHT :draw(10,0);
                }
            }

        void draw(int dx, int dy) {
        start.setLocation(finish.x, finish.y);
        finish.setLocation(start.x + dx, start.y + dy);
        repaint( );
            }
    } // end of the MyListener class

    public void update(Graphics g) {
        paint(g);
    }

    public void paint(Graphics g)
    {
        g.drawLine(start.x, start.y, finish.x, finish.y);
    }
}
```

11

The Abstract Windowing Toolkit

Introduction

If you are used to creating applications in a Windows environment, you will be familiar with the standard Windows components, such as buttons, text boxes and lists. The Abstract Windowing Toolkit (AWT) packages provide a set of classes to allow you to create a GUI interface. These components have events, for example you can click on a button, or change the text in a text box. In this chapter we are going to look at how you create these components and respond to their events.

If you try some of the examples on your computer, they may not appear exactly the same as shown in the figures, since we are not explicitly controlling the positioning of the components. This is controlled by the layout managers which are covered in chapter 12.

Programmers who are used to a Windows specific development environment such as Visual Basic expect to be able to select, drag and resize components at design time. You can do this using the WFC controls to develop Windows specific applications which is covered in chapters 14 and 15, but not with the AWT components.

The AWT class hierarchy

There are two groups of classes, one representing the components such as buttons and list boxes and the other the container classes, which provide a place for the other components to be displayed. In this chapter we are going to look at the visual components. The container classes are covered in chapter 13.

The **Applet** class extends the **Panel** class which extends the **Container** class, therefore applets have an area which can be used to display components. All of the components shown in fig 11.1 extend the **Component** class.

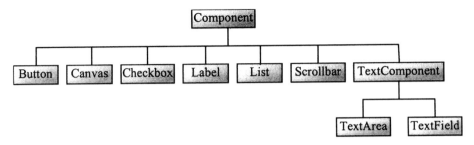

Fig 11.1 *The AWT components.*

The Button Class

The button component will be familiar to every Windows user. To display a button on your applet panel:

- Select the **File | New Project** menu option.
- Select the **New** page, choose the **Web Pages** option.
- Click **Applet on HTML**.

The applet we are going to create is shown in fig 11.2. When you click on the button the text disappears, when you click on it again it appears.

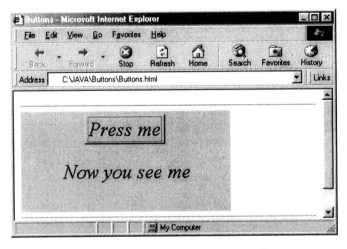

Fig 11.2 *The disappearing text applet.*

We need to import three packages for this applet:

```
import java.applet.*;
import java.awt.*;
import java.awt.event.*;
```

To detect the button click, we need to implement the **ActionListener** interface:

public class Buttons *extends Applet implements ActionListener {*

and then create an instance of the **Button** class:

private Button myButton = new Button("Press me");

The constructor will place the text *Press me* on the button face. To display the button on the panel use the **add** method:

add(myButton);

Next a boolean value called *visible* is created, with an initial value of **true**. When this boolean is **true**, the text is displayed, when it is **false** it disappears.

Since we have implemented the **ActionListener** interface we must override all of the methods of this interface. Fortunately there is only one called **actionPerformed**, which is passed an **ActionEvent** object. In this method, shown below, which is called when the button is clicked, the value of the *visible* boolean is changed and the **repaint** method is called.

```
public void actionPerformed(ActionEvent e) {
    visible = !visible;
    repaint( );
}
```

In **repaint**, the text message *Now you see me* is displayed only if the *visible* boolean is **true**:

```
public void paint(Graphics g) {
// If visible is true display the message otherwise display nothing
    if (visible) g.drawString("Now you see me", 65, 100);
}
```

In the constructor for the *Buttons* class which we have created, the button is added to the panel, the default font size is changed, and a listener is registered for the button:

```
public Buttons( ) {
// Draw the button on the panel
    add(myButton);
    setFont(new Font("TimesRoman", Font.ITALIC, 30));
    myButton.addActionListener(this);
}
```

The complete applet is shown below.

```
import java.applet.*;
import java.awt.*;
import java.awt.event.*;

public class Buttons extends Applet implements ActionListener {
    private Button myButton = new Button("Press me");
    boolean visible = true;

    public Buttons( ) {
```

```
// Draw the button on the panel
        add(myButton);
        setFont(new Font("TimesRoman", Font.ITALIC, 30));
        myButton.addActionListener(this);
        }

    public void actionPerformed(ActionEvent e) {
        visible = !visible;
        repaint( );
    }
    public void paint(Graphics g) {
// If visible is true display the message otherwise display nothing
        if (visible) g.drawString("Now you see me", 65, 100);
    }
}
```

Which button was pressed?

If your applet has more than one button you need to make some additional checks to see which button the event originated from. In the next application there are three buttons, a different text message is displayed depending on which one is pressed. The running applet is shown in fig 11.3.

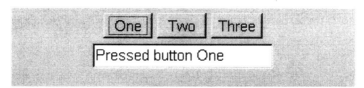

Fig 11.3 *Distinguishing between buttons.*

This applet is similar to the previous example, the **ActionListener** interface is implemented, and three buttons and a **TextField** object are instantiated:

```
public class WhichButton extends Applet implements ActionListener
    {
        private Button one = new Button(" One ");
        private Button two = new Button(" Two ");
        private Button three = new Button("Three");
        private TextField message = new TextField(20);
```

These components are added to the panel in the constructor,

```
public WhichButton( ) {
setFont(new Font("TimesRoman", Font.PLAIN, 15));
// Draw the buttons on the panel
    add(one);
    one.addActionListener(this);
```

```
        add(two);
        two.addActionListener(this);
        add(three);
        three.addActionListener(this);
        add(message);
}
```

A listener is added for each of the buttons. When any of the buttons is clicked the **actionPerformed** method is called:

```
public void actionPerformed(ActionEvent e) {
    String text = "";
    if (e.getSource( ) == one) text = "Pressed button One";
        else if (e.getSource( ) == two) text = "Now button Two";
    else if (e.getSource( ) == three) text = "Finally button Three";
    message.setText(text);
    }
```

To distinguish between the buttons the **getSource** method is used, and the string *text* is assigned a different value. The **setText** method of the **TextField** object is passed the text which it displays.

The complete applet is shown below:

```
import java.applet.*;
import java.awt.*;
import java.awt.event.*;

public class WhichButton extends Applet implements ActionListener
{
    private Button one = new Button(" One ");
    private Button two = new Button(" Two ");
    private Button three = new Button("Three");
    private TextField message = new TextField(20);

    public WhichButton( ) {
    setFont(new Font("TimesRoman", Font.PLAIN, 15));
// Draw the buttons on the panel
        add(one);
        one.addActionListener(this);
        add(two);
        two.addActionListener(this);
        add(three);
        three.addActionListener(this);
        add(message);
    }

    public void actionPerformed(ActionEvent e) {
        String text = "";
        if (e.getSource( ) == one) text = "Pressed button One";
```

```
                     else if (e.getSource( ) == two) text = "Now button Two";
                     else if (e.getSource( ) == three) text = "Finally button Three";
                     message.setText(text);
                     }
            }
```

The Checkbox

The **Checkbox** class is used to display yes/no, true/false options. An example is shown in fig 11.4.

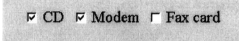

Fig 11.4 Using checkboxes.

These are added to the panel in the same way as button components:

```
import java.applet.*;
import java.awt.*;

public class UsingCheckboxes extends Applet {
private Checkbox cd = new Checkbox("CD");
private Checkbox modem = new Checkbox("Modem");
private Checkbox faxCard = new Checkbox("Fax card");

    public UsingCheckboxes( )
    {
        setFont(new Font("TimesRoman", Font.PLAIN, 20));
        add(cd);
        add(modem);
        add(faxCard);
    }
}
```

All of the checkboxes behave independently, that is any combination may be checked or not checked.

There are five constructors for the **Checkbox** class:

- **Checkbox( )**. A blank **Checkbox** object is created, with the default **false** state.
- **Checkbox(String** label). A **Checkbox** object with the specified label is created.
- **Checkbox(String** label, **boolean** state). The second parameter can be used to explicitly give the **true/false** state. When checked the state is **true**.
- **Checkbox(String** label, **CheckboxGroup** group, **boolean** state). The second parameter indicates which group this checkbox belongs to.
- **Checkbox(String** label, **boolean** state, **CheckboxGroup** group).

If you do not want the checkbox to belong to a group, but you do want to specify its initial state, give it a group of *null*. The effect of a checkbox group is to make the checkboxes interact with other, so that only one member of the group can be set to true. this is useful if only one out of a possible group of actions could apply. A set of **Checkbox** objects in a group are shown in fig 11.5. Only one of this group may be set to **true**, the others are automatically **false**.

Fig 11.5 Using checkbox groups.

These were created using this Java code:

```
import java.applet.*;
import java.awt.*;

public class RadioButtons extends Applet {
private CheckboxGroup pc = new CheckboxGroup( );
private Checkbox slow = new Checkbox("Pentium 233", pc, false);
private Checkbox fast = new Checkbox("PII 300", pc, true);
private Checkbox faster = new Checkbox("PII 400", pc, false);

    public RadioButtons( )  {
        setFont(new Font("TimesRoman", Font.PLAIN, 20));
        add(slow);
        add(fast);
        add(faster);
    }
}
```

When you put checkboxes into a group they change in appearance (when run on a PC) to look like Windows radio buttons.

There are some useful methods of the **Checkbox** class which you need to use checkboxes in your applets and applications:

*Table 11.1 The methods of the **Checkbox** class.*

Method	Description
String getLabel( )	Returns the checkbox label.
boolean getState( )	Returns **true** if the box is checked, **false** if it is not.
void setLabel(String)	Changes the label to the specified string.
void setState(boolean)	Changes the state of the checkbox.
void setCheckboxGroup(CheckboxGroup)	Puts the checkbox into the specified checkbox group. If it is already a member of another group it is removed from that group.

Displaying text

There are three classes which you can use for displaying text:

- The **Label** class. **Label** objects are used for unchanging text.
- The **TextField** class. This class inherits from the **TextComponent** class.
- The **TextArea** class. This class inherits from the **TextComponent** class.

The Label class

The simplest way of displaying text is to use a **Label** component. The text in a label can be changed by your Java code but the user cannot edit it. The **Label** class has three constructors:

- **Label( )**. An empty label is created. If any text is added at run-time it will be left aligned.
- **Label(String)**. A label displaying the specified left aligned text.
- **Label(String, int)**. The second parameter gives the alignment of the text. There are three possible class variables for specifying the alignment of the text: **Label.LEFT, Label.RIGHT, Label.CENTER**.

Fig 11.6 shows a **Label** object.

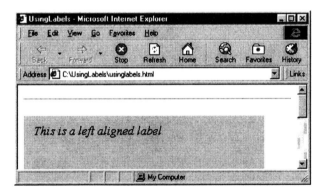

***Fig 11.6** Using **Labels** and **TextField** objects.*

The constructor method used to display this label is shown below:

```
public UsingLabels( ) {
    setFont(new Font("TimesRoman", Font.ITALIC, 20));
    setBackground(Color.lightGray);
    setLayout(new FlowLayout(FlowLayout.LEFT, 10, 10));
    add(new Label(" This is a left aligned label ", Label.LEFT));
}
```

The **Label** class has few methods, the most commonly used ones are shown in table 11.2.

Table 11.2 *The key methods of the* **Label** *class.*

Method	Description
int getAlignment( )	Returns either **Label.LEFT**, **Label.RIGHT** or **Label.CENTER**.
String getText( )	Returns the text of the label.
void setAlignment( )	Sets the alignment of the label.
void setText(String)	Changes the text of the label to the specified string.

The TextField class

The **TextField** component allows you to display or enter a single line of text. This can be edited at runtime by the user or by your Java code. There are four constructors:

- **TextField( )**. Creates a blank text field, zero columns wide.
- **TextField(int)**. Creates a blank text field the specified number of columns wide.
- **TextField(String)**. Creates a text field wide enough to display the supplied text.
- **TextField(String, int)**. Creates a text field of the specified width showing the supplied text.

TextField components are often adjacent to **Label** components which indicate what the text in **TextField** is. In the applet shown in fig 11.7, a name is typed into the two **TextField** components. When the *OK* button is clicked, the welcome is displayed in a third **TextField**. When the *Cancel* button is displayed the text in the **TextField** components is cleared and if there is an existing welcome message it is erased.

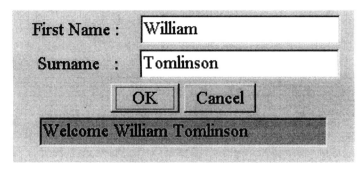

Fig 11.7 Using **Labels** *and* **TextField** *objects.*

The **ActionListener** interface is implemented and the three **TextField** objects are defined as instance variables, along with the other GUI components:

```
public class LabelAndText extends Applet implements ActionListener {
    private Label first = new Label(" First Name : ");
    private TextField name = new TextField(20);
    private Label surname = new Label(" Surname   : ");
```

```
private TextField second = new TextField(20);
private TextField welcome = new TextField(30);
private Button OKButton = new Button(" OK ");
private Button cancelButton = new Button(" Cancel ");
```

They are displayed using the **add** method in the constructor and listeners added for each of the buttons. When either of these buttons is clicked an event occurs. This is trapped by the **actionPerformed** method and a check made to see which of the two buttons has been clicked. If *OK* is clicked, the **String** variable *text* is assigned to the welcome message. The current text in the **TextField** is returned by the **getText** method.

```
public void actionPerformed(ActionEvent e) {
    String text = "";
    if (e.getSource( ) == OKButton)
        text = "Welcome " + name.getText( ) + " " + second.getText( );
    else if (e.getSource( ) == cancelButton) {
        name.setText("");
        second.setText("");
        text = "";
    }
    welcome.setText(text);
}
```

If the *Cancel* button is pressed, the text in the two **TextField** components which represent the first name and surname is cleared by calling the **setText** method for each **TextField** and passing an empty string to it.

The complete applet is shown below:

```
import java.applet. *;
import java.awt. *;
import java.awt.event. *;


public class LabelAndText extends Applet implements ActionListener {
    private Label first = new Label(" First Name : ");
    private TextField name = new TextField(20);
    private Label surname = new Label(" Surname   : ");
    private TextField second = new TextField(20);
    private TextField welcome = new TextField(30);
    private Button OKButton = new Button(" OK ");
    private Button cancelButton = new Button(" Cancel ");

    public LabelAndText( ) {
        setFont(new Font("TimesRoman", Font.PLAIN, 18));
        add(first);
        add(name);
        add(surname);
        add(second);
        add(OKButton);
```

```
                OKButton.addActionListener(this);
                add(cancelButton);
                cancelButton.addActionListener(this);
                add(welcome);
                welcome.setBackground(Color.green);
        }

        public void actionPerformed(ActionEvent e) {
                String text = "";
                if (e.getSource( ) == OKButton)
                        text = "Welcome " + name.getText( ) + " " + second.getText( );
                else if (e.getSource( ) == cancelButton) {
                        name.setText("");
                        second.setText("");
                        text = "";
                }
                welcome.setText(text);
        }
}
```

The most widely used methods are shown in table 11.3. At first glance this list of methods seems to be too brief and does not include methods for selecting, changing or reading text. These methods are defined in the **TextComponent** class, which is a superclass of both **TextField** and **TextArea**.

Table 11.3 *The key methods of the TextField class.*

Method	Description
boolean echoCharIsSet( )	Returns **true** if an echo character is assigned for masked input.
int getColumns( )	Returns the number of columns.
void setEchoChar(char)	Sets the echo character to that specified. This replaces **setEchoCharacter** which is deprecated.
char getEchoChar( )	Returns the current echo character. This replaces **getEchoCharacter** which is deprecated.
void setColumns(int)	Gives the component the specified number of columns.

The most commonly used **TextComponent** methods are listed in table 11.4 and together with the methods defined in **TextField** class itself provide a comprehensive set of methods for text manipulation.

*Table 11.4 The key methods of the **TextComponent** class.*

Method	Description
String getSelectedText( )	Returns the currently selected text.
int getSelectionEnd( )	Returns the end position of the selected area.
int getSelectionStart( )	Returns the start position of the selected area.
String getText( )	Returns the text currently displayed in the component.
void select(int, int)	Selects the text between the start and end position specified.
void selectAll( )	Selects all of the text in the component.
void setEditable(boolean)	If set to **true** the text can be edited. This is the default.
void setText(String)	Over-writes any text in the component with the specified string.

A common use of the **TextField** component is to receive passwords, an application which does this is shown in fig 11.8.

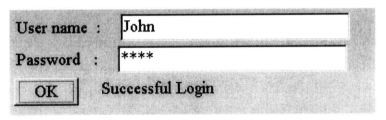

Fig 11.8 Typing a password.

The user name and a password are typed, whatever key is pressed in the password **TextField** a * character appears since the **setEchoChar** method for this component has been used. When the *OK* button is clicked the **actionPerformed** method is called. If the event originated from a button a check is made to see if the user name is *John* and the password is *Borg*. If so the *Successful Login* message is displayed. If an incorrect password or user name is supplied the message *Username or password not recognised* is shown. The complete code for this applet is shown below:

```
import java.applet.*;
import java.awt.*;
import java.awt.event.*;

public class Password extends Applet implements ActionListener {
        private TextField userName = new TextField(25);
        private TextField password = new TextField(25);
        private Button OK = new Button("  OK  ");
        String message;

        public Password( ) {
        setFont(new Font("TimesRoman", Font.PLAIN, 18));
```

```
        setLayout(new FlowLayout(FlowLayout.LEFT));
        add(new Label("User name  : "));
        add(userName);
        add(new Label("Password   : "));
        add(password);
        password.setEchoChar('*');
        add(OK);
        OK.addActionListener(this);
    }

    public void actionPerformed(ActionEvent e) {
        if ((password.getText( ).equals("Borg"))
            && (userName.getText( ).equals("John")))
            message = "Successful Login";
        else message = "Username or password not recognised";
        repaint( );
    }

    public void paint(Graphics g) {
        g.drawString(message, 100, 90);
    }
}
```

Using two listeners

If you want to listen to events produced by a button you need to implement the **ActionListener** interface. If you also wish to act upon events produced by typing text, you also need to implement the **KeyListener** interface or to create an inner class which extends the **KeyAdapter** class.

In the running applet shown in fig 11.9, you can type text into the top TextField component. When you press return, or click on the *OK* button, the text is copied to the lower **TextField** component.

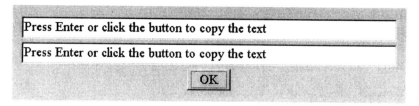

Fig 11.9 *Copying text between* **TextField** *objects.*

The *CopyingText* class implements the **ActionListener** interface and a listener is added for the button. The **actionPerformed** method handles the button click event. The inner class called *MyListener* extends the **KeyAdapter** class and its **keyPressed** method checks to see if the key pressed was the **Enter** key and if so, it does the same as the button click handler. The text in the *in* **TextField** component is found using the **getText** method and is inserted into the *out* **TextField** component using the **setText** method.

```
import java.applet.*;
import java.awt.*;
import java.awt.event.*;

public class CopyingText extends Applet implements ActionListener {
    private TextField in = new TextField(55);
    private TextField out = new TextField(in.getColumns());  //same size as in
    private Button OK = new Button(" OK ");

    public CopyingText(){
        setFont(new Font("TimesRoman", Font.PLAIN, 18));
        add(in);
        add(out);
        add(OK);
        OK.addActionListener(this);
        MyListener m = new MyListener();
        in.addKeyListener(m);
    }

    public void actionPerformed(ActionEvent e) {
        out.setText(in.getText());
    }

    public final class MyListener extends KeyAdapter {
        public void keyPressed(KeyEvent e) {
            if (e.getKeyCode() == KeyEvent.VK_ENTER)
                out.setText(in.getText());
        }
    }//end of MyListener class
}
```

The TextArea class

The **TextArea** class has much in common with the **TextField** class. The **TextField** class only has a single line of text, but the **TextArea** class has a multi-line area with horizontal and vertical scroll bars if required. This class has five constructors:

- **TextArea( )**. Creates an empty area with no columns or rows.
- **TextArea(int** rows, **int** cols). Creates an area with the specified number of rows and columns.
- **TextArea(String** text). Creates a text area large enough to display the specified text.

- **TextArea(String** text, **int** rows, **int** cols). Creates an area containing the text with the specified number of rows and columns.
- **TextArea(String** text, **int** rows, **int** cols, **int** scrollbars). The final parameter determines the type of scrollbars displayed. This can be one of the following values: **TextArea.SCROLLBARS_NONE, SCROLLBARS_VERTICAL_ONLY, SCROLLBARS_HORIZONTAL_ONLY,** or **SCROLLBARS_BOTH.**

This component has a few different methods compared to the **TextField** class as listed in table 11.5, but shares the methods of the **TextComponent** superclass which are listed in table 11.4.

Table 11.5 *The key methods of the **TextArea** class.*

Method	Description
int getColumns( )	Returns the number of columns.
int getRows( )	Returns the number of rows.
void insert(String, int)	Inserts the text starting at the specified position. This replaced the deprecated **insertText** method.
void replaceRange(String, int, int)	The two integer parameters indicate the start and end position of text which is replaced by the supplied text. This method replaces the **replaceText** method which is deprecated.

The List class

When you are designing a GUI it is best to minimize the amount of typing needed. If possible use check boxes or lists so that you can just click on the option you want. The **List** class gives you fully functioning list components. If your list is not big enough to display all of the possible options at once a vertical scrollbar is automatically added. This class has three constructors:

- **List( )**. Creates an empty list. Initially there are no visible lines and only one item can be selected at a time.
- **List(int** rows). Creates a list with the specified number of visible rows.
- **List(int** rows, **boolean** multipleSelections). Creates a list with the specified number of visible rows. If the multipleSelections parameter is **true** more than one item can be selected from the list.

A **List** component as shown in fig 11.10 is used in that applet to change the font of the text displayed below it. To add an item to a list the **addItem** method is used. This method has the name of the font passed to it, and displays it in the list.

Fig 11.10 *Using a List component to change the current font.*

To instantiate the list in this applet:

List theFont = new List(3, false);

This creates a **List** object which will display three lines at a time and does not allow multiple selection. To add the items to the list, use the **addItem** method. To display the list use the **add** method:

theFont.addItem("TimesRoman");
theFont.addItem("Helvetica");
theFont.addItem("Courier");
theFont.addItem("Dialog");
theFont.addItem("ZapfDingbats");
add(theFont);

When you click on a list item it is selected. In this example, since multiple selections are not allowed, only one item may be selected at a time. When an item is selected or deselected, an event occurs. We need to implement the **ItemListener** interface to detect these list events and add a listener for the **List** component called *theFont*:

theFont.addItemListener(this);

When an event occurs the **itemStateChanged** method is called. This is passed an **ItemEvent** object. The **getStateChanged** method returns the event which has occurred if this is a **SELECTED** event, the currently selected item is found using the **getSelectedItem** method which is used to change the font of the **TextField** component. The text displayed in this component is changed to give the current font:

public void itemStateChanged(ItemEvent e) {
*   if (e.getStateChange( ) == ItemEvent.SELECTED) {*
*   text.setFont(new Font(theFont.getSelectedItem( ), Font.PLAIN, 20));*
*   text.setText("The current font is " + theFont.getSelectedItem( ));*
*   }*
}

The complete code for this applet is shown below:

import java.applet.;*
import java.awt.;*
import java.awt.event.;*

```
public class UsingLists extends Applet implements ItemListener {
    private List theFont = new List(3, false);
    private TextField text = new TextField(38);

    public UsingLists() {
        setFont(new Font("TimesRoman", Font.PLAIN, 18));
        theFont.addItem("TimesRoman");
        theFont.addItem("Helvetica");
        theFont.addItem("Courier");
        theFont.addItem("Dialog");
        theFont.addItem("ZapfDingbats");
        add(theFont);
        theFont.addItemListener(this);
        add(text);
    }

    public void itemStateChanged(ItemEvent e) {
        if (e.getStateChange() == ItemEvent.SELECTED) {
            text.setFont(new Font(theFont.getSelectedItem(), Font.PLAIN, 20));
            text.setText("The current font is " + theFont.getSelectedItem());
        }
    }
}
```

The key methods of the **List** class are shown in table 11.6:

*Table 11.6 The key methods of the **List** class.*

Method	Description
void addItem(String)	Adds the string to the list.
void addItem(String, int)	Adds the string to the specified position in the list.
int delItem(int)	Deletes the specified item from the list.
int delItems(int, int)	The parameters specify a start and end position. Items between and including these are deleted.
String getItem(int)	Returns the item at the specified position.
int getItemcount( )	Returns the number of items in the list. This replaces the deprecated **countItems** method.
int getRows( )	Returns the number of visible items.
int getSelectedIndex( )	Returns the index of the selected item. If zero or more than one item selected, -1 is returned.
String getSelectedItem( )	Returns the selected item.
void replaceItem(String, int)	Replaces the item at the specified index with the specified string.
void select(int)	Selects the item at the specified index.

In addition if multiple selection is enabled, there are some methods for managing this as shown in table 11.7.

*Table 11.7 Methods of the **List** class for dealing with multiple selection.*

Method	Description
boolean isMultipleMode( )	If **true** is returned more than one list item may be selected. This method replaces the **allowsMultipleSelections** method which is deprecated.
int[ ] getSelectedIndexes( )	Returns an array of the indexes of the selected items. Only used if multiple selection is enabled.
String[ ] getSelectedItems( )	Returns an array of the selected items. Only used if multiple selection is enabled.
void setMultipleMode(boolean)	If **true** more than one list item may be selected at a time. This method replaces the **setMultipleSelections** method which is deprecated.

The Scrollbar class

Scrollbars are useful components when you want to be able to select from a range of values, perhaps selecting a colour intensity, or moving around a form which is too large to be displayed on your screen.

There are three constructors for the **Scrollbar** class:

- **Scrollbar( )**. Creates a vertical scrollbar.
- **Scrollbar(int** orientation). The orientation must be one of the two possible values, either **Scrollbar.HORIZONTAL** or **Scrollbar.VERTICAL**.
- **Scrollbar(int** orientation, **int** value, **int** visible, **int** minimum, **int** maximum). The orientation specifies if it is horizontal or vertical. The value parameter gives the initial value. The visible parameter is the size of the scrollbar slider. The final two parameters are the minimum and maximum values of the scrollbar.

In some of the Microsoft documentation the term *bubble* is used in preference to *slider*, although this term does not seem to be widely used elsewhere.

The following five methods of this class have been deprecated: **getPageIncrement**, **getLineIncrement**, **getVisible**, **setPageIncrement**, **setLineIncrement**. The updated key methods of the **Scrollbar** class are listed in table 11.8:

*Table 11.8 The key methods of the **Scrollbar** class.*

Method	Description
int getBlockIncrement( )	Returns the change in the position of the slider when clicking between the slider and the arrows at the scrollbar end.
int getMaximum( )	Returns the maximum value of the scrollbar.
int getMinimum( )	Returns the minimum value of the scrollbar.
int getUnitIncrement( )	Returns the change in the position of the slider when the arrows at either end of the scrollbar are clicked.
int getValue( )	Returns the current value.
int getVisibleAmount( )	Returns the width of the slider. This method replaces the **getVisible** method which is deprecated.
void setBlockIncrement(int)	Sets the change in position when clicking between the slider and the end arrow.
void setUnitIncrement(int)	Sets the change in position when clicking on the end arrows.
void setValue(int)	Assigns the specified value and moves the slider to the correct position.
void setValues(int, int, int, int)	Assigns the slider value, the value range represented by the slider, the minimum and maximum values.

In fig 11.11, an applet is shown which allows you to select the red, green and blue components of the rectangle. In this applet, depending on the value of the slider bar, a value of between 0 and 255 is produced.

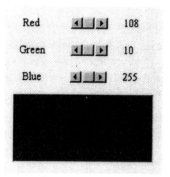

Fig 11.11 Using Scrollbars.

To handle the events which are produced by the scrollbars, you must implement the **AdjustmentListener** interface. The initial value of the red, green and blue components are assigned to the value of the integer constant *initial* (which equals 100).

```
public class UsingScrollbars extends Applet implements AdjustmentListener {
    private static final int initial = 100;
    private Scrollbar redSlider = new
                        Scrollbar(Scrollbar.HORIZONTAL, initial, 20, 0, 255);
    private Scrollbar greenSlider = new
                        Scrollbar(Scrollbar.HORIZONTAL, initial, 20, 0, 255);
    private Scrollbar blueSlider = new
                        Scrollbar(Scrollbar.HORIZONTAL, initial, 20, 0, 255);
```

The same parameter values are supplied for each, they are horizontal scrollbars with an initial value of 100, a slider range of 20, a minimum value of 0 and a maximum value of 255. RGB colours are specified by their red, green and blue intensity. Each colour has an intensity value between 0 and 255, therefore it is straightforward to use the values returned by the slider position to describe the red, green and blue components of a colour.

The **Scrollbar**, **Label** and **TextArea** components are added to the panel. Listeners are added for the three sliders, for example:

```
... ...
add(redSlider);
//add a listener for the red slider
redSlider.addAdjustmentListener(this);
... ...
```

When the position of one of the sliders changes an event occurs which can be trapped by the **adjustmentValueChanged** method, which is passed an **AdjustmentEvent** object:

```
public void adjustmentValueChanged(AdjustmentEvent e) {
// come here when a slider moves
    int red = redSlider.getValue( );
    int green = greenSlider.getValue( );
    int blue = blueSlider.getValue( );
    redIntensity.setText(Integer.toString(red)+ " ");
    greenIntensity.setText(Integer.toString(green) + " ");
    blueIntensity.setText(Integer.toString(blue)+ " ");
// red, green and blue are between 0 and 255
    Color myColor = new Color(red, green, blue);
//set the colour of the TextArea component to the new colour
    t.setBackground(myColor);
    }
```

The current value of each slider is found using the **getValue** method. This will return a value between 0 and 255, since these were assigned as the minimum and maximum values which can be produced by each of the scrollbars. The value returned by each scrollbar is converted into a string value and assigned to the **Label** components adjacent to each scrollbar, giving the new value. A new colour, that is an instance of the **Color** class, called *myColor* is created. The constructor is passed the red, green and blue components of this colour (these components are returned by the slider values).

The **setBackground** method of the **TextArea** component is called using this new colour, so that this component changes colour.

The complete applet is shown below:

```
import java.applet.*;
import java.awt.*;
import java.awt.event.*;


public class UsingScrollbars extends Applet implements AdjustmentListener {
    private static final int initial = 100;
    private Scrollbar redSlider = new
                    Scrollbar(Scrollbar.HORIZONTAL, initial, 20, 0, 255);
    private Scrollbar greenSlider = new
                    Scrollbar(Scrollbar.HORIZONTAL, initial, 20, 0, 255);
    private Scrollbar blueSlider = new
                    Scrollbar(Scrollbar.HORIZONTAL, initial, 20, 0, 255);
    private Label redIntensity = new
                    Label(" " + Integer.toString(initial) + " ");
    private Label greenIntensity = new
                    Label(" " + Integer.toString(initial) + " ");
    private Label blueIntensity = new
                    Label(" " + Integer.toString(initial) + " ");
    private TextArea t = new TextArea(4,25);

    public UsingScrollbars( ) {
        setLayout(new FlowLayout(FlowLayout.CENTER, 20, 10));
        setBackground(Color.yellow);
        setFont(new Font("TimesRoman", Font.PLAIN, 15));
        add(new Label(" Red   "));
        add(redSlider);
//add a listener for the red slider
        redSlider.addAdjustmentListener(this);
        add(redIntensity);
        add(new Label(" Green "));
        add(greenSlider);
//add a listener for the green slider
        greenSlider.addAdjustmentListener(this);
        add(greenIntensity);
        add(new Label(" Blue "));
        add(blueSlider);
//add a listener for the blue slider
        blueSlider.addAdjustmentListener(this);
        add(blueIntensity);
        t.setBackground(new Color(initial, initial, initial));
        add(t);
    }

    public void adjustmentValueChanged(AdjustmentEvent e) {
```

```
// come here when a slider moves
    int red = redSlider.getValue( );
    int green = greenSlider.getValue( );
    int blue = blueSlider.getValue( );
    redIntensity.setText(Integer.toString(red)+ " ");
    greenIntensity.setText(Integer.toString(green) + " ");
    blueIntensity.setText(Integer.toString(blue)+ " ");
// red, green and blue are between 0 and 255
    Color myColor = new Color(red, green, blue);
//set the colour of the TextArea component to the new colour
    t.setBackground(myColor);
    }
}
```

The Canvas class

The **Canvas** class provides a rectangular drawing area. It receives all the events that occur over it. It cannot contain components. There is only one constructor for this component which does not accept any parameters.

If you want to draw on a canvas you must override the default **paint** method. This is done by creating a subclass of **Canvas** with its own **paint** method and using that instead of using **Canvas** directly. This has been done in the applet shown in fig 11.12, a subclass of the **Canvas** class called the *Can* class has been instantiated. The *Can* class has its own **paint** method which can be used to display text or graphics. Each of the two **paint** methods in this application assigns different fonts and texts.

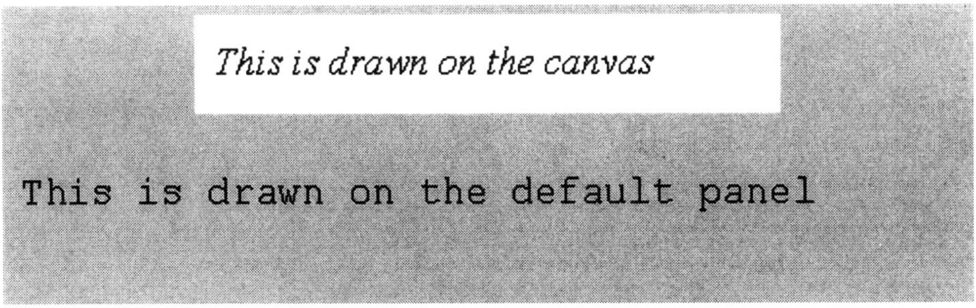

This is drawn on the canvas

This is drawn on the default panel

Fig 11.12 *Using a subclass of **Canvas** class.*

The complete applet is shown below:

```
import java.applet.*;
import java.awt.*;

public class UsingCanvas extends Applet {
    public UsingCanvas( ){
        add(new Can( ));
```

```
        }

    public class Can extends Canvas {
    // extend the Can class and override the its paint class
        public Can( ) {
            setSize(300,50);
            setBackground(Color.white);
        }

        public void paint(Graphics g) {
        // the paint method for the Can class
            setFont(new Font("TimesRoman", Font.ITALIC, 20));
            g.drawString("This is drawn on the canvas", 10, 30);
            }
        }//end of Can class

    public void paint(Graphics g) {
        // the paint method for the UsingCanvas class
        setFont(new Font("Courier", Font.PLAIN, 20));
        g.drawString("This is drawn on the default panel", 10, 100);
    }
}
```

Since a **Canvas** object has no default size, its size is specified using the **setSize** method. It is displayed using the **add** method.

Previewing component layout

A useful feature of this version of Visual J++ is that you can preview the layout of your applet before you run it. Double click on the HTML file in the Project Explorer and the HTML editor is displayed. This has three pages:

- The **Source** page view lists the HTML source code which can be modified.
- The **Design** page shows how the AWT components are set out.
- The **Quick View** page displays a representation of how your web page will look in the browser.

You can use the Toolbox to add HTML components to your HTML code:

- Display the HTML tools on the Toolbox.
- Position the cursor in the HTML code where you want the component to be inserted.
- Double click on the component in the Toolbox to be inserted.

You can see how your Web page will look at run time by showing the **Quick View** page.

12
The Layout Managers

Introduction

In most of the applets and applications we have looked at so far, we have not mentioned how to control the positioning of components on the screen, we have relied on Visual J++ to use defaults, which in the case of applets adds components in a left to right, top to bottom order. If you have tried some of the examples in the previous chapter, you may have found that your programs did not look exactly the same as the figures. This is because you may have specified a different sized applet area in your HTML file, or have a different default font type and size where this is not controlled explicitly in the program.

In this chapter we are going to look at how the layout and positioning of components can be controlled using the layout managers.

Layout policies

The layout policy of a container controls how the components added to it are displayed. If you want to change the layout policy of a container, you have to give the container a class which implements the **LayoutManager** interface using the **setLayout** method.

The standard layout managers are:

- **BorderLayout**.
- **CardLayout**.
- **FlowLayout.**
- **GridLayout**.
- **GridBagLayout**.

We are going to look at each of these layout managers in turn.

The BorderLayout class

This layout class breaks the container area into five regions called **North**, **South**, **East**, **West** and **Center**. When the **add** method is used to add a component to a container using this layout manager, the region must be specified. The centre region fills any space left by the other regions. The **BorderLayout** class is used in fig 12.1.

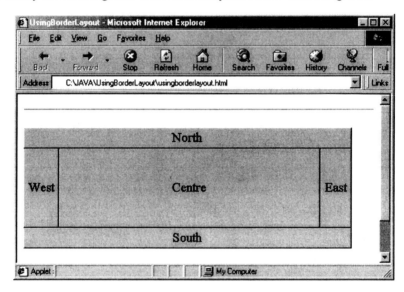

*Fig 12.1 The **BorderLayout** class.*

The applet code is shown below:

```
import java.applet.*;
import java.awt.*;

public class UsingBorderLayout extends Applet {
    public UsingBorderLayout( ){
        setFont(new Font("TimesRoman", Font.PLAIN, 20));
        setLayout(new BorderLayout( ) );
    // The order does not matter
        add("North", new Button("North"));
        add("South", new Button("South"));
        add("East", new Button("East"));
        add("West", new Button("West"));
        add("Center", new Button("Centre"));
        }
    }
```

There are two constructors for this class:

- **BorderLayout( )**. Creates a new border layout.
- **BorderLayout(int** hgap, **int** vgap). Creates a new border layout with the specified horizontal and vertical gaps between components.

Fig 12.2 was produced by exactly the same applet as fig 12.1 except that horizontal and vertical gaps of 30 were specified.

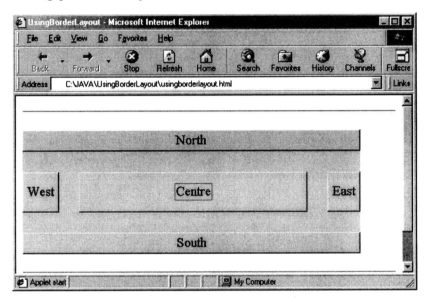

*Fig 12.2 The **BorderLayout** class with large horizontal and vertical gaps.*

The CardLayout class

The **CardLayout** class creates a set of layouts, only one of which is visible at any one time.

There are only two constructors for this class:

- **CardLayout( )**. Creates a new **CardLayout** manager.
- **CardLayout(int** hgap, **int** vgap). Creates a new **CardLayout** manager with the specified horizontal gaps at the left and right edges and the specified vertical gap at the top and bottom edges.

In the applet shown in fig 12.3, there are three layout "cards" each containing a different button. When you click on one button, the next card in the sequence is displayed, which contains another button.

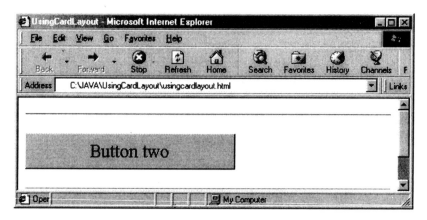

Fig 12.3 The CardLayout class.

The **CardLayout** class is instantiated in the usual way:

CardLayout c = new CardLayout( );

The **setLayout** method is used to assign this layout manager:

setLayout(c);

The buttons are instantiated and added to the layout using the **add** method:

Button first = new Button("Button one");
add("cardOne", first);
first.addActionListener(this);

The first parameter of the **add** method is the name of the card to which the component is to be added. The second parameter is the name of the component. A listener is added to each of the buttons, so that when a button is clicked, the **actionPerformed** method is executed. The button will fill the whole of this card.

To display the card called *cardTwo*, the **show** method is used:

c.show(this, "cardTwo");

Two other buttons are added to two more cards called *second* and *third*. There is nothing special about the names *first*, *second* and *third*, any names could be used.

When a button is clicked this event is trapped in the **actionPerformed** method and the next card is displayed using the **next** method:

c.next(this);

When the last card in the sequence is reached, the next card to be displayed is the first one in the sequence. The complete applet listing is shown below:

import java.applet.*;
import java.awt.*;
import java.awt.event.*;

public class UsingCardLayout extends Applet implements ActionListener {

```
CardLayout c = new CardLayout( );

public UsingCardLayout( ) {
    setFont(new Font("TimesRoman", Font.PLAIN, 25));;
    setLayout(c);
    Button first = new Button("Button one");
    add("cardOne", first);
    first.addActionListener(this);
    Button second = new Button("Button two");
    add("cardTwo", second);
    second.addActionListener(this);
    Button third = new Button("Button three");
    add("cardThree",third);
    third.addActionListener(this);
    c.show(this, "cardTwo");
    }

public void actionPerformed(ActionEvent e) {
// come here when a button is clicked
    c.next(this);
    }
}
```

If you want to add a range of components to a panel and to employ different layouts on each card, a common technique with card layouts is to add a panel to a card and to give that panel its own layout manager. In fig 12.4, a card layout is used with two cards. Each card has a panel added to it. Each of the panels has three buttons on each. The difference in appearance between the two cards is that the panel added to the card shown on the left of fig 12.4 uses the **BorderLayout** class, while the panel added to the other card uses the **FlowLayout** class (which is covered next). Clicking on either panel (not the buttons on the panel) moves to the next card in the sequence.

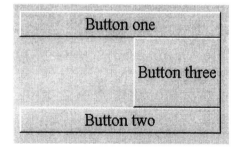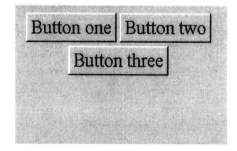

Fig 12.4 Using FlowLayout and BorderLayout with the CardLayout class.

The code listing for this applet is shown below:

```
import java.applet. *;
import java.awt. *;
import java.awt.event. *;
```

```
public class CardLayoutWithPanels extends Applet implements MouseListener {
    CardLayout c = new CardLayout( );

    public CardLayoutWithPanels( ) {
        setFont(new Font("TimesRoman", Font.PLAIN, 25));
        setLayout(c);
// create panelOne and add it to CardOne
        Panel panelOne = new Panel( );
        panelOne.setLayout(new BorderLayout( ));
        panelOne.add("North", new Button("Button one"));
        panelOne.add("South", new Button("Button two"));
        panelOne.add("East", new Button("Button three"));
// add this panel to CardOne
        add("CardOne", panelOne);
// add a mouse listener for panelOne
        panelOne.addMouseListener(this);
// create panelTwo and add it to cardTwo
        Panel panelTwo = new Panel( );
        panelTwo.setLayout(new FlowLayout( ));
        panelTwo.add(new Button("Button one"));
        panelTwo.add(new Button("Button two"));
        panelTwo.add(new Button("Button three"));
// add this panel to CardTwo
        add("CardTwo", panelTwo);
// add a mouse listener for panelTwo
        panelTwo.addMouseListener(this);
        c.show(this, "CardOne");
    }

    public void mousePressed(MouseEvent e) {
// if either panel is clicked display the next card
        c.next(this);
    }
    public void mouseReleased(MouseEvent e) { }
    public void mouseEntered(MouseEvent e) { }
    public void mouseExited(MouseEvent e) { }
    public void mouseClicked(MouseEvent e) { }
}
```

Some of the most commonly used methods of this class are shown in table 12.1.

Table 12.1 *The key methods of the **CardLayout** class.*

Method	Description
first(Container)	Displays the first card in the sequence.
last(Container)	Displays the last card.
next(Container)	Displays the next card, or the first if the last card is currently displayed.
previous(Container)	Displays the previous card or the last if the first card is currently displayed.
show(Container, String)	Displays the card with the specified name. If an invalid name is given, no action is taken.

The FlowLayout class

This is the default layout class for Java applets. Components are added to the container from left to right. When the first row is filled, a new row is started.
Fig 12.5 shows the **FlowLayout** class in use.

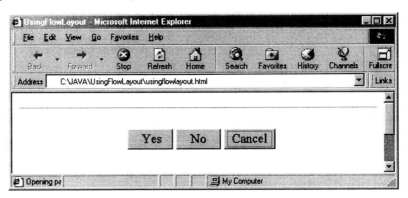

Fig 12.5 The FlowLayout class.

The code required to produce this applet is shown below. If the container area is not wide enough for all three of the buttons, they may appear on separate lines.

```
import java.applet.*;
import java.awt.*;

public class UsingFlowLayout extends Applet {

    public UsingFlowLayout() {
        setFont(new Font("TimesRoman", Font.PLAIN, 20));
        setBackground(Color.white);
        setLayout(new FlowLayout(FlowLayout.RIGHT));
```

```
    add(new Button(" Yes "));
    add(new Button(" No "));
    add(new Button(" Cancel "));
    }
}
```

There are three constructors for this class:

- **FlowLayout( )**. Creates a new flow layout manager with a horizontal and vertical gap of 5 pixels between components.
- **FlowLayout(int align)**. Creates a new flow layout manager with the specified alignment and a 5 pixel horizontal and vertical gap. The alignment must be either **FlowLayout.LEFT, FlowLayout.RIGHT** or **FlowLayout.CENTER**
- **FlowLayout(int align, int hgap, int vgap)**. Creates a new flow layout manager of the specified alignment with the specified gaps.

The three different alignments are shown in fig 12.6. Note that whatever alignment is used, the components are added in the same order.

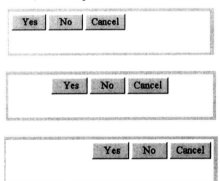

Fig 12.6 Left, centre and right alignment.

The GridLayout class

This layout manager breaks the container into a rectangular grid. Each of the grid cells is the same size. This class has two constructors:

- **GridLayout(int rows, int cols)**. Creates a grid layout with the specified number of rows and columns.
- **GridLayout(int rows, int cols, int hgap, int vgap)**. Creates a grid layout with the specified number of rows and gaps with horizontal and vertical gaps between the cells.

Fig 12.7 shows the **GridLayout** class in action.

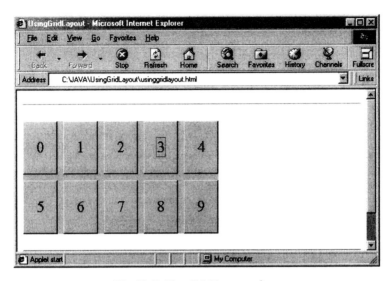

*Fig 12.7 The **GridLayout** class.*

The code used to create this applet is shown below:

```
import java.applet.*;
import java.awt.*;

public class UsingGridLayout extends Applet {

    public UsingGridLayout(){
        int c;
        setFont(new Font("TimesRoman", Font.PLAIN, 25));
        setLayout(new GridLayout(2, 5, 10, 10));
        for (c = 0; c <=9; c++)
            add(new Button(String.valueOf(c)));
    }
}
```

The **valueOf** method of the **String** class converts the integer *c* into a string representation so that it can be displayed on the face of the button.

The GridBagLayout class

This layout manager is the most flexible of the layout classes but is also the most difficult to use. The display area is divided into an array of rectangular cells in the same way as for the **GridLayout** class, the difference is that components may occupy one or more adjacent cells. Every component which is added to a **GridBagLayout** has a **GridBagConstraints** object associated with it, which controls aspects of how the component is laid out. The sequence that you have to follow when using the **GridBagLayout** class is as follows:

- Create an instance of the **GridBagLayout** class.
- Create an instance of the **GridBagConstraints** class.
- Define the values of the instance variables of the **GridBagConstraints** object.
- Create an instance of the component to be added.
- Associate the component with the **GridBagConstraints** object, using the **setConstraints** method of the **GridBagLayout** class.
- Add the component to the layout.

To add another component, you can either create a new instance of the **GridBagConstraints** class or change the instance variables of the existing **GridBagConstraints** object and then associate it with the component as before.

The **GridBagLayout** class is more complex to use than the other layout classes, in particular because of the associated **GridBagConstraints** class which we need to look at first.

Table 12.2 The variables of the GridBagConstraints class.

Field	Description
anchor	Determines where the component is placed. This field has one of the following possible values: **CENTER, NORTH, NORTHEAST, EAST, SOUTHEAST, SOUTH, SOUTHWEST, WEST,** or **NORTHWEST**. The default is **CENTER.**
fill	Determines how to resize the component. There are four possible values: **NONE**, the component is not resized. **BOTH**, the component entirely fills the display. **HORIZONTAL**, the component is made wide enough to fill the container. **VERTICAL**, the component is made tall enough to fill the container. The default is **NONE**.
gridheight	The number of cells in a column for the display area. The default value is 1.
gridwidth	The number of rows for the display area. The default is value is 1.
gridx	The number of the cells on the left of the component. The leftmost cell has a **gridx** value of 0. A value of **RELATIVE** adds the component on the right of the previously added component. The default is **RELATIVE**.
gridy	The number of the cell at the top of the component, where the topmost cell has a **gridy** value of 0. A value of **RELATIVE** add the component directly below the previously added component. The default is **RELATIVE**.
weightx	If the width of a layout is smaller than the width of the container, the **weightx** value determines how to distribute the remaining space. A component with a **weightx** of 2.0 will have twice the space allocated compared to a component with a **weightx** of 1.0.
weighty	If the height of a layout is smaller than the height of the container, the **weighty** value determines how to distribute the remaining vertical space.

Fig 12.8 shows the **GridBagLayout** in use. The whole of the display area is filled since the **fill** property of the **GridBagConstraints** object is **BOTH**.

Button one occupies the entire width of the display area and is about half the height of buttons two and three, since it has a **weighty** value of 1.0 compared to 2.0. Note that a **weighty** of 2.0 does not mean that the height will be twice that of a component with a **weighty** of 1.0. It does mean that any extra space left after the default height of the components has been considered will be divided in a 2:1 ratio.

Button *three* is about two thirds the width of button *two*, since it has a **weighty** value of 2.0 compared to 3.0.

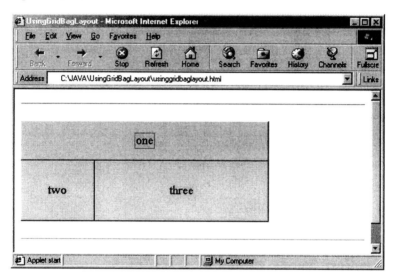

Fig 12.8 The GridBagLayout class.

The complete code for this applet is given below:

```
import java.applet.*;
import java.awt.*;

public class UsingGridBagLayout extends Applet {
    public UsingGridBagLayout( ) {
    setFont(new Font("TimesRoman", Font.PLAIN, 20));
    GridBagLayout g = new GridBagLayout( );
    setLayout(g);

    GridBagConstraints gc = new GridBagConstraints( );
// resize the components to fill the entire horizontal and vertical space.
    gc.fill = GridBagConstraints.BOTH;
    gc.weightx = 1.0;
    gc.weighty = 1.0;

    Button buttonOne = new Button("one");
// this gridwidth will make the button occupy the entire width
```

```
        gc.gridwidth = GridBagConstraints.REMAINDER;
        g.setConstraints(buttonOne, gc);
        add(buttonOne);

        Button buttonTwo = new Button("two");
// This weighting means that components will be taller than in the previous row.
        gc.weightx = 2.0;
        gc.weighty = 2.0;
        gc.gridwidth = GridBagConstraints.RELATIVE;
        g.setConstraints(buttonTwo, gc);
        add(buttonTwo);

        Button buttonThree = new Button("three");
        gc.weightx = 3.0;
        gc.gridwidth = GridBagConstraints.REMAINDER;
        g.setConstraints(buttonThree, gc);
        add(buttonThree);
        }
    }
```

13

The Container Class

Introduction

Since all applets extend the **Applet** class which extends the **Panel** class, which in turn extends the **Container** class, applets can be used to display visual components. If you are writing an application which does not extend the **Applet** class, you do not have a container for any visual components you wish to use and will have to create your own.

Many applets and applications need to have more than one container. For example, you may wish to display a dialog box containing a warning or some useful information. It is also useful to be able to create a menu system. You can do all of this using a set of subclasses of the **Container** class to create both applets and applications with a powerful graphical interface.

The Container class

The **Container** class and its subclasses is shown in fig 13.1. It is an abstract superclass of all the classes which can hold components.

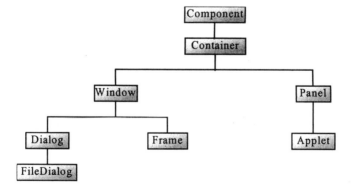

Fig 13.1 *The container components.*

The **Window** class, although not an abstract class, is rarely used directly, and its sub classes are generally used instead.

The Panel class

The **Panel** class is the simplest of the container classes. It only has one constructor with no parameters. You can add other components to a panel, including other panels.

Any events which occur over the panel are sent to it. Its default layout manager is **FlowLayout**. An example of displaying a label on a panel is shown in fig 13.2.

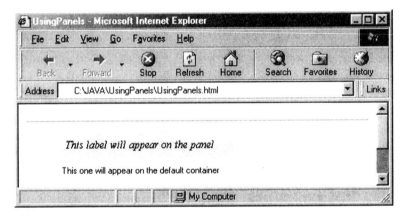

Fig 13.2 *The **Panel** class.*

The Java code used to produce this applet is shown below:

```
import java.applet.*;
import java.awt.*;

public class UsingPanels extends Applet {

    public UsingPanels( ) {
        setBackground(Color.white);
        Panel p = new Panel( );
// set the panel colour to yellow and the font to italic
        p.setBackground(Color.yellow);
        p.setFont(new Font("TimesRoman", Font.ITALIC, 14));
        p.add(new Label("This label will appear on the panel "));
// add the panel (containing the label) to the default container
        add(p);
        add(new Label("This one will appear on the default container "));
    }
}
```

The Frame class

A frame has a title and a border. Its default layout manager is **BorderLayout**. Frames are usually used in applications as a container for displaying components, but they can be used within an applet and run within the browser environment.

There are two constructors for the **Frame** class:

- **Frame( )**. Creates a new frame with no title.
- **Frame(String)**. Create a new frame with the specified title.

Fig 13.3 shows an applet which has a single button, when this button is clicked a frame is displayed with a **Label** component.

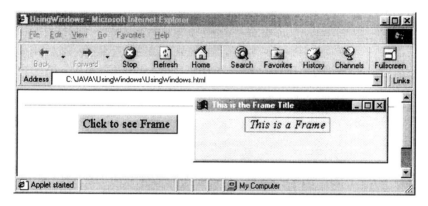

Fig 13.3 *Displaying frames.*

This class implements the **ActionListener** interface. In its constructor the background area is set to white, the font to 18-point Times Roman and a button is displayed. A listener is added to the button.

When the button is clicked the **actionPerformed** method is called:

```
public void actionPerformed(ActionEvent e) {
    if (myFrame != null) { //if the frame already exists destroy it
        myFrame.setVisible(false);
        myFrame.dispose( );
    }
    ...........
```

A check is made to see if the frame exists (to avoid creating a new frame every time the button is clicked). If it does exist, it is made invisible and all system resources associated with it are released. This is an important check, since without it, every time you clicked on the button a new frame would be created. It is not strictly necessary to make the frame invisible before calling the **dispose** method, however some Java programs include this because of a bug in earlier versions.

The next stage is to create the new frame:

```
myFrame = new Frame(" This is the Frame Title");
myFrame.setLayout(new FlowLayout(FlowLayout.CENTER));
```

```
            myFrame.add(new Label(" This is a Frame "));
            myFrame.setSize(300,100);
            myFrame.setBackground(Color.yellow);
            myFrame.setFont(new Font("TimesRoman", Font.ITALIC, 18));
            myFrame.setVisible(true);
            }
```

An instance of the **Frame** class is created with the title *This is the Frame Title* displayed on its title bar. It is assigned the **FlowLayout** manager, a label is added to it, it is resized, its **Background** colour changed, its font is changed and finally it is displayed using the **setVisible** method. The **setVisible** method has a boolean parameter, if this is **true** the frame is made visible. This method replaces the **show** and **hide** methods which will still work, but are now deprecated.

The complete listing for the applet is shown below:

```
        import java.applet.*;
        import java.awt.*;
        import java.awt.event.*;

        public class UsingWindows extends Applet implements ActionListener{
            private Frame myFrame;

            public UsingWindows() {
                setBackground(Color.white);
                setFont(new Font("TimesRoman", Font.PLAIN, 18));
                Button showFrame = new Button("Click to see Frame ");
                add(showFrame);
                showFrame.addActionListener(this);
            }

            public void actionPerformed(ActionEvent e) {
                if (myFrame != null) { //if the frame already exists destroy it
                    myFrame.setVisible(false);
                    myFrame.dispose();
                }
                myFrame = new Frame(" This is the Frame Title");
                myFrame.setLayout(new FlowLayout(FlowLayout.CENTER));
                myFrame.add(new Label(" This is a Frame "));
                myFrame.setSize(300,100);
                myFrame.setBackground(Color.yellow);
                myFrame.setFont(new Font("TimesRoman", Font.ITALIC, 18));
                myFrame.setVisible(true);
            }
        }
```

Before you use the **setVisible** method to display a frame, you need to use the **setSize** method to specify its size, if you do not only the title bar will be visible. The **setSize** method replaces the **resize** method which is now deprecated.

If you want to write an applet which displays a frame and has events which have to be handled, the usual way is to add a class to the applet which extends the **Frame** class and implements the **ActionListener** interface.

In fig 13.4 an applet is shown which is a development of the previous applet. When the button labelled *Click to show Frame* is clicked, a frame is displayed. When the button on that frame or the close icon in the top right corner is clicked that frame is destroyed. This applet uses two classes, *UsingFrames* which extends **Applet** and *Second* which extends **Frame**.

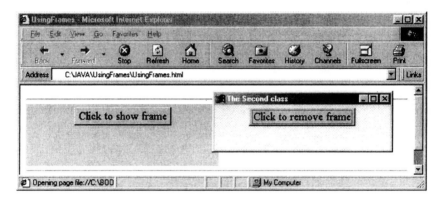

Fig 13.4 Handling Frame events.

The constructor method for the *UsingFrames* class displays a single button. When you click on this the **actionPerformed** method is called as in the previous example. The *UsingFrames* class is shown below:

```
import java.applet.*;
import java.awt.*;
import java.awt.event.*;

public class UsingFrames extends Applet implements ActionListener {
private Second myFrame;

    public UsingFrames( )  {
        setFont(new Font("TimesRoman", Font.PLAIN, 18));
        Button showFrame = new Button("Click to show frame");
        add(showFrame);
        showFrame.addActionListener(this);
    }

    public void actionPerformed(ActionEvent e) {
    //if the frame already exists destroy it
        if (myFrame != null) {
            myFrame.dispose( );
        }
    // display a new frame
        myFrame = new Second(Color.yellow);
```

```
        }
    }
```

In the **actionPerformed** method a check is made to see if the frame already exists, if it does it is destroyed. A new instance of the *Second* class is instantiated. The constructor for this class is passed a **Color** object.

The *Second* class implements the **ActionListener** interface. In its constructor, the title *The Second class* is added to the frame. Its background is assigned to the colour passed to the constructor, in this case yellow. The **FlowLayout** manager is used, a new button is added to the frame, which is resized and displayed. A listener is added to this button. When this button is clicked the **actionPerformed** method is called:

```
public void actionPerformed(ActionEvent e) {
// the button has been clicked so close the frame
    dispose( );
}
```

This method destroys the frame.

There is one further refinement which has been added to this applet. In a Windows environment if you click on the icon in the top right of a window, it is closed. To achieve the same effect we need to trap the window destroy event and remove the frame as a result of this event occurring.

To catch windows events we need to either implement the **WindowListener** interface or extend the **WindowAdapter** class. In this case we use an inner class to extend the **WindowAdapter** class. Both the class and interface contain seven methods, if we chose to use the interface we would have to include six empty methods, since we only wish to handle the window closing event. When you click on the close icon of the window the **windowClosing** method is called. The inner class is shown below:

```
public class ClosingWindow extends WindowAdapter {
//the close icon on the frame has been clicked
    public void windowClosing(WindowEvent e) {
        dispose( );
    }
}// end of ClosingWindow class
```

The Java code for the *Second* class and this inner class is shown below:

```
import java.applet.*;
import java.awt.*;
import java.awt.event.*;

class Second extends Frame implements ActionListener {

    Second(Color c) {
        setTitle("The Second class");
        setFont(new Font("TimesRoman", Font.PLAIN, 18));
        setBackground(c);
        setLayout(new FlowLayout(FlowLayout.CENTER));
        Button b = new Button("Click to remove frame");
```

```
        add(b);
        b.addActionListener(this);
        setSize(300,100);
        setVisible(true);
        ClosingWindow close = new ClosingWindow( );
        addWindowListener(close);
    }

public void actionPerformed(ActionEvent e) {
// the button has been clicked so close the frame
    dispose( );
}

public class ClosingWindow extends WindowAdapter {
//the close icon on the frame has been clicked
    public void windowClosing(WindowEvent e) {
        dispose( );
    }
    }// end of ClosingWindow class
}
```

There are seven methods of the **WindowListener** interface (and the **WindowAdapter** class), which are shown in table 13.1.

Table 13.1 *The methods of the WindowListener interface.*

Method	Description
windowActivated(WindowEvent)	Invoked when a window is activated.
windowClosed(WindowEvent)	A window has been closed.
windowClosing(WindowEvent)	A window is being closed, you can override the close operation.
windowDeactivated(WindowEvent)	A window is being deactivated at this point.
windowDeiconified(WindowEvent)	A window is converted from an icon to an open window.
windowIconified(WindowEvent)	A window is being converted to an icon on the toolbar.
windowOpened(WindowEvent)	A window has been opened.

The Dialog class

Dialogs are designed to be temporary windows that display helpful information and in some cases allow you to specify which of a range of options you want. Dialog boxes can either be modal or modeless, a modal dialog does not allow you to do anything else in the application until you have responded to it. The default layout manager is **BorderLayout**.

The **Dialog** class has two constructors:

- **Dialog(Frame, boolean)**. You must attach a dialog to a frame. If the boolean is **true**, the dialog is modal, otherwise it is modeless.
- **Dialog(Frame, String, boolean)**. The String parameter ensures that a title bar is added with the specified title.

Dialogs, like frames, are invisible until the **setVisible** method is called with its single boolean parameter assigned to **true**.

The next application shows a typical use of dialog boxes. The running application is shown in fig 13.5. In the frame on the left, two integer values are typed into the top two text fields, when the button is clicked the sum is displayed in the third text field. If a non-integer is typed, the dialog on the right is displayed and input field is cleared. To close the application, click on the close icon in the top right corner of the frame.

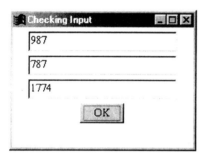 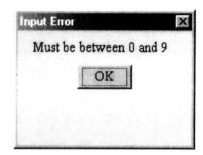

Fig 13.5 Displaying a Dialog when an error occurs.

The application defines a class called *UsingDialogs*. It starts in the usual way in the main method by instantiating an instance of this class:

```
public static void main(String args[ ]) {
    UsingDialogs f = new UsingDialogs("Checking Input");
}
```

The *UsingDialogs* class extends the **Frame** class and implements both the **ActionListener** and the **KeyListener** interfaces.

The constructor does the usual setting up of the application, defining the layout managers and fonts, and adding the components to the frame. The dialog which displays the error message is also instantiated here, and the warning message and a button are added to it, but it is not displayed. Six listeners are added in the constructor:

- Two key listeners are added for the two text fields where the numbers are typed. The *UsingDialogs* class implements the **KeyListener** interface, therefore all three methods in this interface, **keyReleased**, **keyTyped** and **keyPressed** must be added, although only the **keyReleased** method is used to detect each character as it is typed and to display the error dialog if an invalid character is typed.
- Two action listeners are added for the button on the frame and the button on the dialog. The **ActionListener** interface only has one method, **actionPerformed** which is implemented.

- Two windows listeners are added to deal with the closing of the frame and dialog. These are implemented using an inner class called *Close* which extends the **WindowAdapter** class. Only the **windowClosing** method is implemented. Since we are extending a class rather than implementing an interface there is no need to override all of the methods in the **WindowAdapter** class.

We are going to look at each of these listeners in more detail. The **keyReleased** method is shown below:

```
public void keyReleased(KeyEvent e) {
// if a digit, new line, backspace, enter or an action key is typed
// take no action otherwise display the error dialog
// and clear the input line
if ((Character.isDigit(e.getKeyChar( )) == false) &&
    (e.isActionKey( ) == false) &&
    (e.getKeyCode( ) != KeyEvent.VK_ENTER) &&
    (e.getKeyCode( ) != KeyEvent.VK_BACK_SPACE) &&
    (e.getKeyCode( ) != KeyEvent.VK_DELETE)) {
        if (e.getSource( ) == text1) text1.setText("");
        else text2.setText("");
        d.setVisible(true);
        }
}
```

The only valid characters are the digits 0→9 and keys which are used to edit the number, that is, the action keys such as the arrowed keys, the enter, backspace and delete keys. If the key which has been pressed is not one of these, a check is made using the **getSource** method to see which text field the character was typed in, and that field is cleared using the **setText** method.

When one of the buttons is clicked the **actionPerformed** method is called. If the button clicked was on the dialog, the dialog is made invisible. If the button on the frame was clicked, the text typed into the top two text fields is converted to an integer, they are added together and the result converted back to a string which is placed in the bottom text field.

```
public void actionPerformed(ActionEvent e) {
// if the button on the dialog has been clicked close the dialog
    int value1, value2;
        if (e.getSource( ) == dialogButton)
            d.setVisible(false);
// if the OK button on the main window has been clicked add the numbers
        else if (e.getSource( ) == okButton) {
        value1 = Integer.parseInt(text1.getText( ));
        value2 = Integer.parseInt(text2.getText( ));
        text3.setText(String.valueOf(value1 + value2));
    }
}
```

The closing of the frame and the dialog is handled by the inner class called *Close*. If possible it is better to extend the **WindowAdapter** class rather than the corresponding **WindowListener** interface since they have seven methods and often only one or two are required. In this application only the **windowClosing** event is used:

```
public class Close extends WindowAdapter {
// the close icon has been clicked, if it's on the dialog close it
// if it's on the main window close the application.
    public void windowClosing(WindowEvent e) {
        if (e.getSource( ) == d) d.dispose( ); else //close the dialog
        System.exit(0);           //end the application
    }
} //end of the Close class
```

If the close icon which was clicked was on the dialog, the dialog is removed. If the close icon on the frame was clicked the application is ended.

Error checking in an application is a major undertaking. This application does not cope with floating point or negative numbers, it makes no check to ensure that the numbers are not large, but it is still several times the size of a comparable application which has no error checking. The completed application is shown below:

```
import java.awt.*;
import java.awt.event.*;


class UsingDialogs extends Frame implements ActionListener, KeyListener {

    private TextField text1 = new TextField(25);
    private TextField text2 = new TextField(25);
    private TextField text3 = new TextField(25);
    private TextField answer = new TextField(20);
    private Button okButton = new Button(" OK ");
    private Button dialogButton = new Button(" OK ");
    private Dialog d = new Dialog(this, "Input Error", true);

    public UsingDialogs(String title) {
        setTitle(title);
        setSize(250,300);
        setFont(new Font("TimesRoman", Font. PLAIN,15));
        setLayout(new FlowLayout(FlowLayout.CENTER));
        add(text1);
        text1.addKeyListener(this);
        add(text2);
        text2.addKeyListener(this);
        add(text3);
        add(okButton);
        okButton.addActionListener(this);
        setVisible(true);
        d.setSize(200, 150);
        d.setBackground(Color.yellow);
```

```
        d.setLayout(new FlowLayout(FlowLayout.CENTER));
        d.add(new Label(" Must be between 0 and 9 "));
        d.add(dialogButton);
        dialogButton.addActionListener(this);
        Close c = new Close( );
        addWindowListener(c);
        d.addWindowListener(c);
}

public void keyReleased(KeyEvent e) {
// if a digit, new line, backspace, enter or an action key is typed
// take no action otherwise display the error dialog
// and clear the input line
if ((Character.isDigit(e.getKeyChar( )) == false) &&
        (e.isActionKey( ) == false) &&
        (e.getKeyCode( ) != KeyEvent.VK_ENTER) &&
        (e.getKeyCode( ) != KeyEvent.VK_BACK_SPACE) &&
        (e.getKeyCode( ) != KeyEvent.VK_DELETE)) {
            if (e.getSource( ) == text1) text1.setText("");
            else text2.setText("");
            d.setVisible(true);
            }
}
public void keyTyped(KeyEvent e) {
}
public void keyPressed(KeyEvent e) {
}

public class Close extends WindowAdapter {
//  the close icon has been clicked, if it's on the dialog close it
//  if it's on the main window close the application.
        public void windowClosing(WindowEvent e) {
            if (e.getSource( ) == d) d.dispose( ); else  //close the dialog
            System.exit(0);               //end the application
        }
} //end of the Close class

public void actionPerformed(ActionEvent e) {
// if the button on the dialog has been clicked close the dialog
        int value1, value2;
            if (e.getSource( ) == dialogButton)
                d.setVisible(false);
// if the OK button on the main window has been clicked add the numbers
            else if (e.getSource( ) == okButton) {
            value1 = Integer.parseInt(text1.getText( ));
            value2 = Integer.parseInt(text2.getText( ));
            text3.setText(String.valueOf(value1 + value2));
```

```
            setVisible(true);
        }
    }

    public static void main(String args[ ]) {
        UsingDialogs f = new UsingDialogs("Checking Input");
    }
}
```

The FileDialog class

The **FileDialog** class displays a system-dependent dialog which is used for accessing files. The dialog for Windows is shown in fig 13.6.

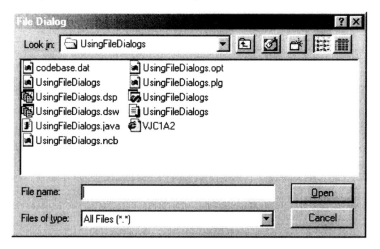

*Fig 13.6 The **FileDialog** class.*

There are three constructors for this class:

- **FileDialog(Frame)**. Creates a file dialog.
- **FileDialog(Frame, title)**. Creates a file dialog with the specified title.
- **FileDialog(Frame, String, int)**. The integer parameter can be either of two possible values, **FileDialog.LOAD** or **FileDialog.SAVE**, which indicates whether the dialog is to be used for loading or saving a file.

The **setVisible** method is used to display the dialog.

Since there are restrictions on applets accessing the local file system, this dialog is only likely to be used in applications. The most useful methods of this class are shown in table 13.2.

Table 13.2 *Frequently used methods of the **FileDialog** class.*

Method	Description
String getFile( )	Returns the name of the currently selected file, or null if no file is selected.
String getDirectory( )	Returns the currently selected directory.
FilenameFilter getFilenameFilter( )	Specifies which type of files will appear in the file dialog.
int getMode( )	Indicates if the dialog is to be used for saving or loading a file, the returned value is either **FileDialog.LOAD** or **FileDialog.SAVE**.
void setDirectory(String)	Changes the current directory to the one specified.
void setFile(String)	Changes the current file to the one specified.
void setFilenameFilter(FilenameFilter)	Changes the filter to the one specified, which determines which types of files are displayed.

This dialog does not actually save or load any files, it is simply a way of finding the file you want or of specifying the location and name of a file which is to be saved. To use files you will need to use the stream classes of Java which are covered in chapter 19.

Using menus

Menus are an integral part of many applications or applets which use frames. The AWT package provides a comprehensive set of classes and methods for controlling all aspects of menus. Fig 13.7 shows a frame with a menu.

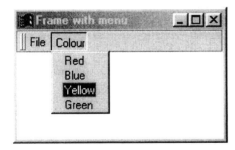

Fig 13.7 Using menus.

- Create a new instance of the **MenuBar** class.
- Add the menu bar to your frame using its **setMenuBar** method.
- Create an instance of the menu you want, this corresponds to a menu heading.
- Add items to each menu using the **add** method.

To create the menu bar and add it to a frame as shown in fig 13.7:

```
MenuBar m = new MenuBar( );   // create a new menu bar
setMenuBar(m);                 // add to the frame
```

To create an instance of the menu:

```
Menu file = new Menu("File");
```

To add this menu to the menubar using the **add** method:

```
m.add(file);
```

Add each item to the menu:

```
file.add(new MenuItem("Open"));
file.add(new MenuItem("Close"));
file.add(new MenuItem("Save"));
file.add(new MenuItem("Save As"));
```

If you want to add another menu to the same menu bar, you create the menu and add items to it as before:

```
Menu colour = new Menu("Colour");
m.add(colour);
colour.add(new MenuItem("Red"));
colour.add(new MenuItem("Blue"));
colour.add(new MenuItem("Yellow"));
colour.add(new MenuItem("Green"));
```

The listener is added not to the individual menu items but to the menu itself, in this case:

```
colour.addActionListener(this);
```

Finally the frame is displayed using the **setVisible** method:

```
setVisible(true);
```

The Java code for this application, apart from the **actionPerformed** method (which is described in the next section) is shown below:

```
import java.awt.*;
import java.awt.event.*;

public class UsingMenus {
    public static void main(String args[ ]) {
        MenuFrame frameWithMenu = new MenuFrame("Frame with menu");
    }
}

class MenuFrame extends Frame implements ActionListener {
    MenuFrame(String title) {
        setFont(new Font("TimesRoman", Font.PLAIN, 18));
```

```
    setTitle(title);
    setSize(300,200);

    //create a menu bar
    MenuBar m = new MenuBar( );
    setMenuBar(m);

    // instantiate the "File" object and add to the menu bar
    Menu file = new Menu("File");
    m.add(file);
    // add the menu items to the "File"
    file.add(new MenuItem("Open"));
    file.add(new MenuItem("Close"));
    file.add(new MenuItem("Save"));
    file.add(new MenuItem("SaveAs"));
    // instantiate the "Colour" object and add to the menu bar
    Menu colour = new Menu("Colour");
    m.add(colour);
    colour.addActionListener(this);
    // add a listener to the colour menu
    colour.add(new MenuItem("Red"));
    colour.add(new MenuItem("Blue"));
    colour.add(new MenuItem("Yellow"));
    colour.add(new MenuItem("Green"));
    //display the frame
    setVisible(true);
}
```

Handling menu events

To handle the events which occur when you select a menu you must implement the **ActionListener** interface. The events are handled by the **actionPerformed** method. In the **actionPerformed** method shown below a check is made to see which menu item the event originated from by comparing the text of the menu items. When a match is found the background is changed to the corresponding colour. The frame is hidden and shown again to ensure that the changed colour takes effect.

```
public void actionPerformed(ActionEvent e) {
    String command = e.getActionCommand( );
    if (command.equals("Red")) setBackground(Color.red);
    else if (command.equals("Blue")) setBackground(Color.blue);
    else if (command. equals("Yellow")) setBackground(Color.yellow);
    else if (command.equals("Green")) setBackground(Color.green);
    setVisible(false);        // hide and then redraw
    setVisible(true);         // with the new background colour
}
```

Sub-menus, separators and other menu features

In addition to adding menu items to a menu you can add separator lines. To do this add an item with a label of "-":

MenuItem sep = new MenuItem("-");

If you create a menu and add it to an existing menu, the one you add becomes a sub-menu as shown in fig 13.8.

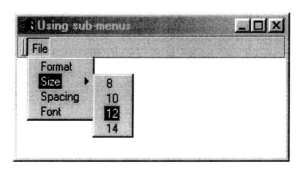

***Fig 13.8** Using sub-menus.*

To create the *File* menu as before create a menu bar and add it to the frame:

MenuBar m = new MenuBar( );
setMenuBar(m);

Create the *File* menu and add it to the menu bar:

Menu file = new Menu("File");
m.add(file);

Add the *Format* item to the menu:

file.add(new MenuItem("Format"));

To add the *Size* item to the menu, create a menu called *size* and add items to it:

Menu size = new Menu("Size");
size.add(new MenuItem("8"));
size.add(new MenuItem("10"));
size.add(new MenuItem("12"));
size.add(new MenuItem("14"));

To make *size* a sub-menu add it to the *file* menu:

file.add(size);

Finally add the two remaining items:

file.add(new MenuItem("Spacing"));
file.add(new MenuItem("Font"));

If you want to create Windows applications, you can use the Windows Foundation Classes and an excellent visual development environment. We look at in the next chapter.

14

The Windows
Foundation Classes

Introduction

One of the most significant developments in version 6 of Visual J++ is the ability to use the Windows Foundation Classes (WFC) for Java. This is a powerful set of class libraries which helps you to build applications to run specifically in a Microsoft Windows environment. In addition to Windows .EXE files you can also create ActiveX controls. Visual J++ includes a powerful visual environment for creating these applications, which will look very familiar to Visual Basic programmers.

The applications you develop using the WFC will not be portable and will only run in a Windows environment. Many purists think this is counter to the basic philosophy of Java, which is to produce portable, machine independent applications, but in practice, there has been demand to use Java to write fast efficient applications for Windows and the WFC allows you to do this. For the first time Java can be viewed as a serious alternative to Visual C++ for writing Win32 applications.

Virtually all of the WFC controls are defined in classes which extend the **Control** class in the **com.ms.wfc.ui** package. The controls which are used to access a relational database which are in the **com.ms.wfc.data.ui** package, and other controls such as the **Timer** are in the **com.ms.wfc.app** package. Even though many of the classes and methods have similar or identical names to the classes and methods defined in the **java.awt** packages, Java is able to distinguish between because you have to explicitly state which packages you wish to import.

Creating a Windows application

To create a Win32 application:

- Select the **File | New Project** option from the menu. The window shown in fig 14.1 will be displayed.
- Select the **Windows Application** option as shown.
- Specify the name and location of the file.

- Click on the **Open** button. If there is a currently open project, you will be asked if you wish to save it.

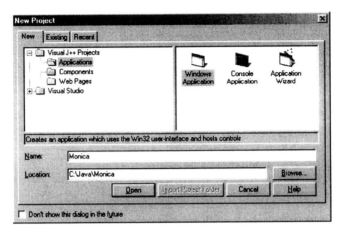

Fig 14.1 *Creating a Win32 application.*

If you wish to include extra items such as a menu to your application you can select the **Application Wizard** option, which is covered later in this chapter.

The application you have created will appear similar to that shown in fig 14.2, although there will be some differences depending on how you have configured your development environment.

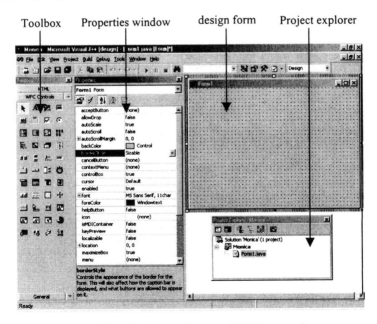

Fig 14.2 *The design form and WFC controls.*

To create Win32 applications you will need to use the design form, the Toolbox and the Properties box. If the Toolbox or the Properties window are not displayed you should select the **View | Toolbox** and the **View | Properties Window** menu option.

If the design form is not shown select the **View | Project Explorer** menu option as shown in fig 14.3 and double click on the name of the form, in this case *Form1.java*.

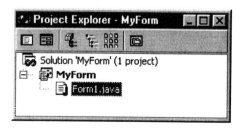

Fig 14.3 The Project Explorer.

Using the application wizard

If you wish to add a menu to your project you can use the application wizard. Choosing the **File | New Project** menu, display the **New** page, choose the **Application** folder and select the **Application Wizard** icon. This will display the window shown in fig 14.4.

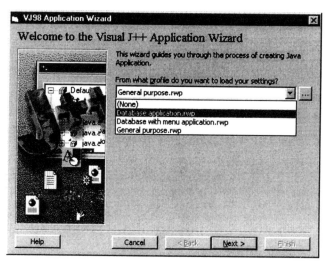

Fig 14.4 Selecting the profile.

The only choice you have to make at this stage is the profile you wish to use. A profile is a file which contains the options you have selected from running the wizard on a previous occasion. At the end of running the wizard you can save the settings you have chosen as a profile file, which will then be available for you to use in later sessions. In this example choose **(None)**. Click on the **Next** button to go to the next window, shown in fig 14.5.

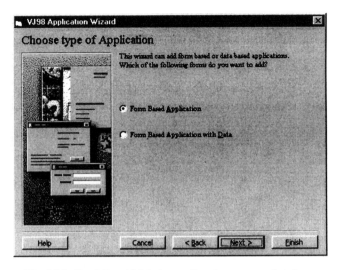

Fig 14.5 Deciding if this is application uses a database.

The default option on this window is **Form Based Application**, which will create an application with a single window. If you choose the **Form Based Application with Data** option, the Data Form Wizard is launched which produces a form based application which is linked to the fields in a single table of a database. Supported databases are Microsoft Access and those databases which can be referenced through ODBC. The Data Form Wizard is covered in chapter 20. In this example choose the default **Form Based Application** option.

There are some common features listed in fig 14.6 which you can add to your application.

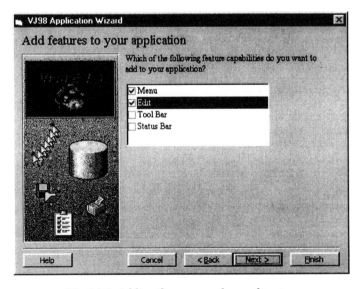

Fig 14.6 Adding features to the application.

- The **Menu** option adds a standard menu with typical File, Edit and Help options.
- **Edit** adds an **Edit** component to the application and some Java code. When the application is run this component fills the form and the application produced behaves like the Windows Notepad application.
- **Toolbar** adds a toolbar and some standard buttons.
- **Status Bar** adds a status bar to the form.

In this example choose the **Menu** and **Edit** options. Click on **Next** to proceed to the following stage, shown in fig 14.7.

You can choose the number of comments that are added to your initial application. The first few times that you run the wizard it is a good idea to include all of the possible comments. When you are more familiar with the code which is produced you will probably want to include the minimum of these automatically generated comments. In this case make sure that all three of the check boxes are checked to include all of the available comments.

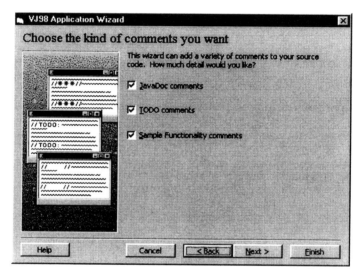

Fig 14.7 Adding comments to the application.

Click on the **Next** button to display the following window shown in fig 14.8. Visual J++ offers a range of different types of files which can be produced for distribution. If you want to produce a standalone Windows executable file choose the **EXE file** option. If you want to produce class files which will run within the virtual Java machine environment choose the **Class files** option. The **Cabinet (CAB) file** option compresses all the class files produced into a single file for archiving or ease of distribution. Click on the **Next** button to proceed.

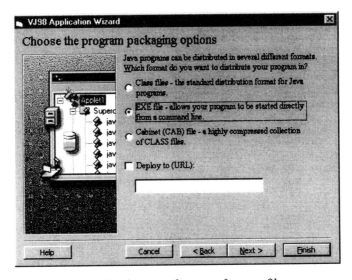

Fig 14.8 Choosing the type of output files.

The final window displayed by the wizard allows you to save the choices that you have made in a Wizard profile file as shown in fig 14.9. Click on the button with three dots on its face, adjacent to the list box to display the Save Profile dialog.

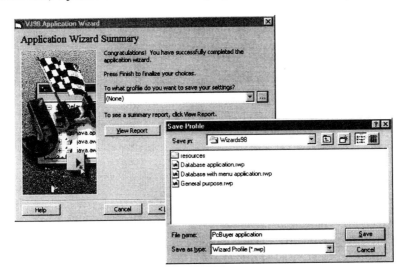

Fig 14.9 Saving a profile and finishing the application generation.

If you want a summary of the choices that you have made, click on the **View Report** button to produce the window shown in fig 14.10.

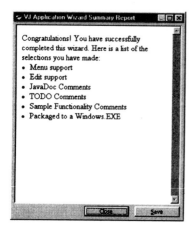

Fig 14.10 The Wizard summary report.

Close the summary report and finally click on the **Finish** button to complete the application.

The completed application is shown in fig 14.11. It consists of a single form, an **Edit** component and a **MainMenu** component. There are some standard menu items, but you can add your own by typing them in any of the places indicated by the **Type Here** text. When the application is run, the **Edit** component completely fills the window and the menu commands and supporting Java code which is produced by the Wizard makes the running application behave like the Window's Notepad application. You can type, select, cut, paste and copy text. You can also open a text file and it will be displayed and you can also save text to a file.

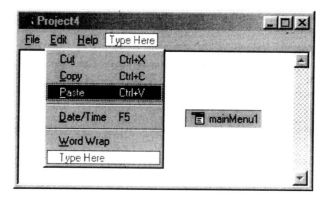

Fig 14.11 The completed application.

The application is run in the same way as usual – the easiest way is to click on the **Run** button on the toolbar. The running application is shown in fig 14.12.

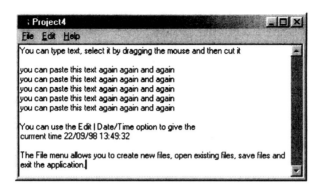

Fig 14.12 The running Notepad application.

The applications produced by the wizard are not intended to be complete, you will need to make changes and additions to get the application you want, but hopefully the wizard will do some of the standard, routine aspects of the application for you.

WFC controls

Many of the WFC controls are similar in appearance and behaviour to the AWT components defined in the AWT package, but the WFC controls are Windows specific. The key WFC controls are shown in table 14.1.

All of the WFC controls are in the **wfc.ui** package, but you can create your own controls either by extending the functionality of existing controls or by creating completely new ones.

Adding controls to the design form

If you are writing a Windows application you will usually start by using the **File | New Project** menu option and choosing either the **Windows Application** or **Application Wizard** option. However you start, you will need to add additional WFC controls to your form and to move and resize these controls.

To add a control:

- Select the control that you wish to add from the Toolbox.
- Move to the design form and press the left mouse button and drag. The point where you press the button is either the top left or the bottom right of the control.
- The control you have chosen in the Toolbox is automatically de-selected.
- Select the next control you wish to add and repeat the process.

If you wish to add more than one control of the same type ensure that the **Ctrl** key is pressed when you select a control from the Toolbox. After adding the control to the form the control will not be de-selected.

Table 14.1 *Key WFC controls.*

Control	Name	Description
	Pointer	When this control is selected you can resize, move and select controls.
A	**Label**	Displays static text, usually used to indicate the purpose of an adjacent control.
ab	**Edit**	Allows multi-line text to be input and edited.
ab	**Button**	When this control is clicked some action is taken.
	Checkbox	A control used when a true/false response is required.
	RadioButton	A control used to indicate true/false response, usually used as part of a group in which only one can be set.
xv	**GroupBox**	A container which holds other controls in a group. This control has a text field in the top left corner.
	Panel	The simplest container class, which provides an area for other components, including panels to be placed.
	ComboBox	This control can be used in three forms. A drop-down combo box including an editable text line, a drop-down list with read-only text and a simple combo which is the same as a drop-down combo except that it is always in a drop-down state.
	ListBox	A scrolling list of text items, which can be configured so that one or more items can be selected.
	CheckedListBox	An extension to the standard **ListBox**. Check boxes are placed adjacent to each item and methods are provided which check and set the state of these boxes.
	HScrollBar	A horizontal scroll bar.
	VScrollBar	A vertical scroll bar.
	PictureBox	A container for a picture.
	Timer	A control which triggers an event at regular intervals. The time between events is configurable.

Moving and resizing controls

Usually when you are designing a form you will not get the size, position and alignment of the components right at the first attempt. Fortunately it is straightforward to make changes. To move or resize controls they must be selected. There are three ways of doing this:

- If you only want to select one control, click on it; clicking on another control automatically de-selects the first.
- If you want to select more than one control and they are located closely together, you can click the mouse in a position which will become a corner of a rectangle when the mouse is dragged enclosing the controls you wish to select.
- If the controls you want to select are spread widely across the form and it is not possible to enclose them in a rectangle by dragging the mouse, you can select the component with the **Ctrl** key pressed, this will not de-select controls which have previously been selected.

When controls are selected they will have eight sizing handles as shown in fig 14.13. To change the size of a control drag on one of the handles. If you have selected more than one control, dragging on any of the handles will resize all of the controls.

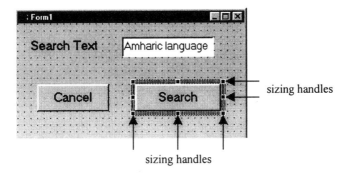

Fig 14.13 Sizing handles on selected controls.

To move selected controls drag the controls to the new position (make sure that you do not drag one of the sizing handles).
To delete selected controls press the **Delete** key.

Changing control properties at design time

You can change the properties of the components and forms at design time by using the Properties window. To display this window select the **View | Properties Window** menu option or press **F4**. The properties of the currently selected components are shown. If you select more than one component only properties which all the selected components have are displayed. The Properties window is shown in fig 14.14.

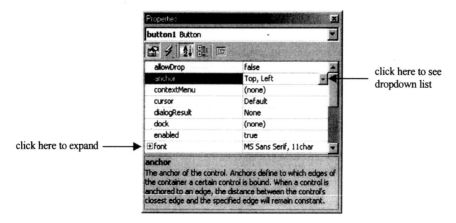

Fig 14.14 The Properties window.

You can display the properties and events of a selected component in a variety of ways using the four icons at the top of the Properties window as shown in fig 14.15.

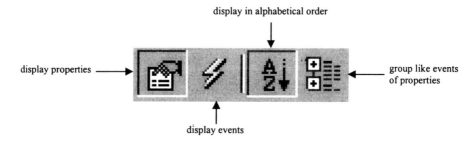

Fig 14.15 Changing the display of the Properties window.

You can display either events or properties and also choose whether the display is in alphabetical order or the items are grouped with similar items.

Some properties have a small number of pre-defined possible values, for example the **visible** property can only be **true** or **false**. These properties have a down facing arrow on the right of the current property value which you can click on to see the available options.

You are required to type the value for other properties, for example the **text** property of a button, that is the text displayed on the button face, must be typed if you do want to use the default text.

Properties which have a + sign adjacent to them are compound properties which will expand when clicked, for example the **font** property is composed of the **name**, **size**, **weight**, **italic underline** and **strikeout** properties. When the tree is expanded, the positive sign is converted to a – sign, which causes the tree to collapse when it is clicked.

A few properties such as the **Lines** property of **Edit** objects, have a button with three dots on the right of the property value. Click on this button to run the String List Editor, which allows you to enter multi-line text.

If you change an object's property in the Properties window that change is immediately effective. If, for example, you change the **font** property, all text associated with that object automatically changes. There are methods in each class for finding out the values of these properties and changing them at run-time. Each control has many properties (even a simple button has 26) fortunately although you may wish to change a few properties, such as the **enabled** property at run-time, many of the properties relate to the appearance and position of the control and it is unlikely that you will often wish to change them.

Customizing the Toolbox

In addition to the controls covered in this chapter there are many additional controls which are supplied with Visual J++ and hundreds are available from software companies. You can even create your own. If you want to customize the Toolbox choose the **Tools | Customize Toolbox** menu option as shown in fig 14.16. You can choose from ActiveX, WFC or Applets. When you have chosen the control you want to add, click on its checkbox and then on the **OK** button. It is automatically added to your Toolbox.

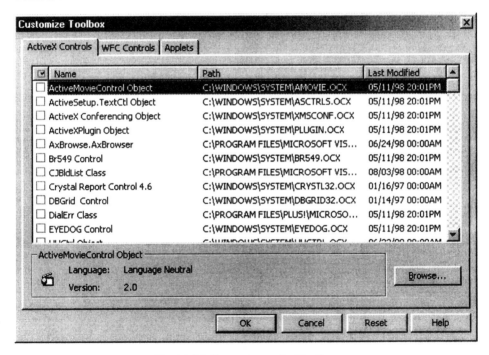

Fig 14.16 Customizing the Toolbox.

Aligning controls

For your applications to look professional the positioning of the components is critical. It is usually best to show the grid, which appears as a matrix of dots, on the design form and to make your controls snap to these grid points. This is the default, but can be altered using the **Tools | Option** menu option and displaying the **Form Designer | WFC** page. The **Format** menu has an extensive set of tools for aligning components.

Table 14.2 Aligning components.

Icon	Description
Lefts	Aligns components to the left border of the first component selected.
Centers	Ensures that the vertical centres are aligned.
Rights	Ensures that right borders are aligned.
Tops	Ensures that the tops are aligned.
Middles	Ensures that the horizontal centres are aligned.
Bottoms	Ensures that the bottoms are aligned.
to Grid	Moves the control so that its top left corner snaps to the nearest grid point.

The **Format | Align** menu options are shown in table 14.2. When a group of components are aligned, it is the last control they are aligned to, that is, the last control does not move.

If you are adding several components of the same type to a form it is often important to ensure that they are all the same size. The **Format | Make Same Size** menu option has three options shown in table 14.3 which does this for you.

Table 14.3 Changing size.

Icon	Description
Width	Gives all the selected controls the same width as the first selected control.
Height	Gives all the selected controls the same height.
Both	Gives all selected controls the same width and height.

The **Format** menu has several further options for organizing and repositioning controls as shown in table 14.4.

*Table 14.4 Further options in the **Format** menu.*

Icon	Description
⬚ Size to Grid	Adjusts the size of the control so that it is an exact number of grid squares.
Horizontal Spacing	There are four options for adjusting the horizontal spacing. **Make Equal** ensures that the horizontal spacing between three or more controls is equal. The **Increase** and **Decrease** options change the spacing between controls. The spacing does not have to be equal to use these two options. The **Remove** option butts controls horizontally against each other.
Vertical Spacing	The same as the previous option, but in a vertical direction.
Center in Form	The selected control can be moved either to the vertical or horizontal centre of the form.
Order	Two options: **Bring to Front** and **Send to Back**, which control the positioning of overlapping controls.
🔒 Lock Controls	Fixes a control's position so that it cannot be moved.

Using the WFC

The visual interface for creating Windows-based interfaces is easy to use to create an effective user-interface, but to create fully functioning applications we need to look in more detail at properties of the controls and how to handle the events which these controls can produce. We are going to do this in the next chapter.

15

Using the Windows Foundation Classes

Introduction

If you are writing applications which will run specifically on a Windows PC it is very likely that you will use the Windows Foundation Classes. The WFC has been widely used by Windows programmers for several years and has good performance and a high degree of functionality. Most of the things that you can do using the WFC can be achieved using the Abstract Windowing Toolkit, but the AWT is not as mature and does not have as extensive a range of classes and methods as the WFC. The main benefit of using the AWT is that your application will be portable to any platform. Portability was one of the main reasons why Java gained such wide acceptance, so it does seem odd Microsoft have included the facility to write Windows specific code. However, it is a facility which will be used and help Java to make further inroads into application areas where developers would previously have used Visual C++.

In the previous chapter we looked at how you create a Windows application and briefly looked at some of the most widely used controls. In this chapter we are going to look in more detail at the key methods and properties of these controls and see how to handle the events which these controls can produce.

The Control class

All WFC controls extend the **Control** class and therefore inherit the methods and variables of that class. This is a huge class, the description in the on-line help is over 100 pages long. Many of the methods are related to handling mouse and keyboard events which we look at later in this chapter. A few of the most commonly used methods are given in table 15.1.

*Table 15.1 Common methods of the **Control** class.*

Method	Description
getEnabled( )	Returns a boolean indicating if the control is enabled or not.
getFont( )	Returns a string indicating the current font.
getSize( )	Returns the size of the control as a **Point** object. The **Point** class has two variables **x** and **y** which in this case give the width and height.
getText( )	Returns the **text** property as a string, for example in the case of an **Edit** control this method returns the text displayed.
setEnabled(boolean)	If the parameter is true the control is enabled.
setFont(Font)	Changes the font to that specified.
setSize(int width, int height)	Changes the size of the control to the specified width and height.
setText(String)	Changes the **text** property to the string specified.
setVisible(boolean)	If the boolean is **true** the control is visible, if **false** it is made invisible. This method replaces the **show** and **hide** methods which are now deprecated.

The Font class

One class which is very often used is the **Font** class which is in the **wfc.ui** package and it encapsulates a Win32 class. This should not be confused with the **Font** class which is in the **java.awt** package. This class has a comprehensive set of fourteen constructors, the most commonly used ones are:

- **Font(String** name, **float** size, **int** units, **int** weight, **boolean** italic, **boolean** underline, **boolean** strikeOut). This creates a new font with the specified characteristics.
- **Font(String** name, **float** size). Creates a font with the specified font face and size.
- **Font(Font** font, **float** size, **int** units, **int** weight, **boolean** italic, **boolean** underline, **boolean** strikeOut). This creates a new font with the specified characteristics.
- **Font(Font** font, **float** size, **int** units). Creates a font based on an existing font, but with different sized characters.

The weight and size must be one of the constants defined in the **FontWeight** and **FontSize** classes respectively. The **Font** class has some defined font names to help you to produce portable applications, which use the fonts which the user has specified for his system rather than explicitly naming a font such as Courier or Helvetica. These are shown in table 15.2:

Table 15.2 *Using portable fonts.*

Name	Description
ANSI_FIXED	Standard ANSI fixed width font.
ANSI_VAR	Standard ANSI variable width font.
DEFAULT_GUI	The default font used by the current user interface.
DEVICE_DEFAULT	The default font used by the current graphics device.
OEM_FIXED	The standard original (OEM) fixed width font.
SYSTEM	The standard Windows variable width system font.
SYSTEM_FIXED	The standard Windows fixed width system font.

The seven fonts for my system are shown in fig 15.1 in the order they are listed in table 15.2..

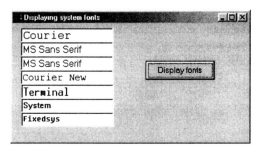

Fig 15.1 *Displaying system fonts.*

The Java code used to create this application is shown below:

```
public class Form1 extends Form {
    private void button1_click(Object sender, Event e)
    {
    change(edit1, Font.ANSI_FIXED);
    change(edit2, Font.ANSI_VAR);
    change(edit3, Font.DEFAULT_GUI);
    change(edit4, Font.DEVICE_DEFAULT);
    change(edit5, Font.OEM_FIXED);
    change(edit6, Font.SYSTEM);
    change(edit7, Font.SYSTEM_FIXED);
    }

    private void change(Edit e, Font myFont) {
        e.setFont(new Font(myFont, 20, FontSize.PIXELS));
        e.setText((e.getFont()).getName());
    }
// the Visual J++ generated code follows from here
```

The method *change* takes two parameters, the **Edit** object whose text is to be changed and the name of the font. The text in the **Edit** object is assigned to be the name of the font. The **getFont** method returns the font of the **Edit** object and the **getName** method returns the face name of the font as a **String** object.

In addition to the **getName** and **getFont** methods the **Font** class has many methods which return information on a **Font** object. The most commonly used ones are shown in table 15.3.

Table 15.3 *Methods of the* **Font** *class in the* ***coms.ms.wfc.ui*** *package.*

Name	Description
getBold( )	Returns a boolean value, true if the font is bold, otherwise false.
getCharacterSet( )	Returns an integer which is an enumerated **wfc.app.CharacterSet** value, which identifies the current character set.
getFontMetrics( )	Returns a **FontMetrics** object with full details of the characteristics of the font.
getItalic( )	Returns a boolean value, **true** if the font is bold, otherwise **false**.
getSize( )	Returns the font size in points as a integer.
getStrikeout( )	Returns a boolean value, **true** if the characters are struck out, that is, have a horizontal line drawn through them.
getUnderline( )	Returns a boolean value, **true** if the font is underlined, otherwise **false**.
getWeight( )	Returns an enumerated integer value defined in the **FontWeight** class, which gives the boldness of the font. The higher the value the bolder the font.

There are no methods for changing characteristics of a font in the **Font** class, if you want to change the font of a control, which is a subclass of the **Control** class, you can use the methods defined in the **Control** class. This is shown later in this chapter in the section covering the **Button** class.

Handling events

Visual J++ greatly simplifies the process of handling events which originate from the WFC controls. Each event for each component has an event handler associated with it. When the event occurs, the handler is automatically executed.

If you want to create an outline event handler:

- Select the control whose events you want to handle.
- Display the events list for that control on the Properties window.
- Double click on the event you want to handle in the left column of the Properties window.
- The outline event handler is created as an empty method, as shown in fig 15.2.
- Add your Java code to this method.

click here to display events

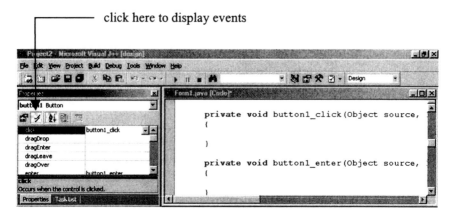

Fig 15.2 Create an event handler.

The event handler methods created are always of the same form, for example the click event handler for a **Button** object called *button1*:

private void button1_click(Object sender, Event e)
{
// put your Java code to handle the event here
}

The method is always **private void**. Its name is made up of three components: the name of the object; an underscore character; the name of the event.

The parameters which are passed to the method vary depending on the event. The first is always an **Object** identifying the sender.

The Label and Edit classes

Both of these controls are used to display text, the difference is that the **Label** objects displays text which is unchanging, while **Edit** objects are used for you to input your own text. In fig 15.3 the text *Username* and *Password* are **Label** objects, while the controls where the username and password are typed are **Edit** objects.

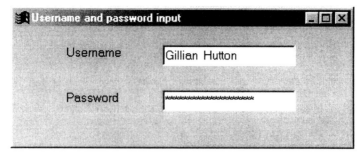

*Fig 15.3 Using **Label** and **Edit** objects.*

Note that the password **Edit** control displays only the * character irrespective of which character on the keyboard is pressed. This is achieved by setting the **passwordChar** property to *. The **text** property of the control still contains the actual text typed – and not just a row of * characters.

The **Label** and **Edit** classes share many properties, the most widely used are shown in table 15.4.

Table 15.4 *Common properties of the **Label** and **Edit** classes.*

Property	Description
enabled	If this property is **true** the control is available for use. If it is **false** the control is disabled and usually drawn in a paler colour than that used for enabled controls.
font	This property is made up of several sub properties: **name, size weight, italic, underline** and **strikeout** which each control different aspects of the font.
name	This is the name of the object and is used in your application to refer to that object. The default name for the first **Label** object is *label1*, the second is called *label2* and so on. The first **Edit** object is called *edit1*.
text	This is the text which is displayed in the **Label** or in a single line **Edit** object. It is easy to confuse this with the **name** property since the default text is always the same as the default name.
visible	If this property is **true** the control can be seen and used, if it is **false** it is invisible and disabled.

In addition the **Edit** control has some extra properties compared to the **Label** control, the most commonly used of these properties are shown in table 15.5:

Table 15.5 *Additional properties of the **Edit** class.*

Property	Description
lines	In a multi-line **Edit** object this property contains the text displayed. The default is **false**.
multiline	If this is **true**, more than one line of text may be displayed. The default is **false.**
passwordChar	The character which is displayed whenever any key is pressed.
readOnly	If this property is **true** the text displayed in the **Edit** object cannot be changed. The default is **false**.
scrollBars	You can choose: **None, Horizontal, Vertical** or **Both**. The default is **None**.

If you click on the button adjacent to the value of the **Lines** property, the String List Editor as shown in fig 15.4 is displayed, and you can type the text as you wish it to appear in the **Edit** control. All of these properties can be controlled at runtime using the corresponding get and set methods, for example **getVisible()** and **setVisible**(boolean) read and change the **Visible** property.

Fig 15.4 *The String List Editor.*

The Button class

The **Button** class is used to initiate some action. When a **Button** object is clicked a click event occurs. In the application shown in fig 15.5, when the *Italic/Non Italic* button is clicked the text changes between italic and plain. When the *Bigger* and *Smaller* buttons are clicked the text changes size.

To create this application:

- Create a new Windows application.
- Add an **Edit** object to the design form and change the **text** property to *Chameleon*.
- Add a **Button** object to the form and change its **text** property to *Italic/Non italic*. This changes the text on the button face.
- Add two other buttons and change their **text** properties to *Bigger* and *Smaller* so that your application looks like the one shown in fig 15.5.

Fig 15.5 *Changing fonts.*

The next stage is to add the event handlers for the **Button** objects and some Java code to change the displayed text.

The quickest way to create the event handler for a button is to double click on it. This creates the method shown:

```
private void button1_click(Object sender, Event e)
{
    ... ...
}
```

To change the size of the font of the control which we have left with the default name *edit1*, we need to use the **setFont** method of the **Control** class, which is the superclass of the **Edit** class. This method is passed a **Font** object. The constructor for the **Font** object we are creating requires the name of the font, its size, weight, and three booleans indicating if the font is in italics, underlined and struck out. Since we want to leave all aspects of the font unchanged apart from whether it is italicized or not, the **getName, getSize, getUnits, getWeight, getItalic, getUnderline** and **getStrikeout** methods get the current values of these properties. The not operator '!' is used to change the state of the boolean parameter which controls whether the font is in italics or not between **true** and **false**. The code which does this is shown below:

```
private void button1_click(Object source, Event e)
{
edit1.setFont(new Font((edit1.getFont()).getName(),
                       (edit1.getFont()).getSize(),
                       (edit1.getFont()).getUnits(),
                       (edit1.getFont()).getWeight(),
                       !((edit1.getFont()).getItalic()),
                       (edit1.getFont()).getUnderline(),
                       (edit1.getFont()).getStrikeout()));
}
```

The effect of this Java code, which is executed every time that the click event for a button occurs, is to change the text in *edit1* between a plain and an italic font.

The methods which handle the click events for the buttons with *Bigger* and *Smaller* on their faces also use the **setFont** method, but the constructor for the **Font** method which is used is different, and only requires the name of the current font, which is returned by the **getFont** method and a second parameter which is the new size of the font. The current size is obtained from the **getSize** method and increased or decreased by 1, depending on which button is clicked. The first part of the completed application, including the methods which handle the click events from the three buttons is shown below:

```
import com.ms.wfc.app.*;
import com.ms.wfc.core.*;
import com.ms.wfc.ui.*;
/**
 * This class can take a variable number of parameters on the command
 * line. Program execution begins with the main() method. The class
 * constructor is not invoked unless an object of type 'Form1' is
 * created in the main() method.
 */
```

```
public class Form1 extends Form {
// constructor for Form1 and the dispose method produced by J++ not shown
    private void button1_click(Object source, Event e) {
    edit1.setFont(new Font((edit1.getFont( )).getName( ),
                            (edit1.getFont( )).getSize( ),
                            (edit1.getFont( )).getUnits( ),
                            (edit1.getFont( )).getWeight( ),
                            !((edit1.getFont( )).getItalic( )),
                            (edit1.getFont( )).getUnderline( ),
                            (edit1.getFont( )).getStrikeout( )));
    }
    private void button2_click(Object source, Event e) {
        edit1.setFont(new Font(edit1.getFont( ),
                            (edit1.getFont( )).getSize( ) + 1,
                            (edit1.getFont( )).getUnits( )));
    }
    private void button3_click(Object source, Event e) {
        edit1.setFont(new Font(edit1.getFont( ),
                            (edit1.getFont( )).getSize( ) - 1,
                            (edit1.getFont( )).getUnits( )));
    } // J++ generated code follows here
```

The CheckBox, RadioButton and GroupBox classes

The **CheckBox** class is used when you want to offer a range of options, as shown in fig 15.6. Any number of checkboxes may be checked. Note that the **CheckBox** class in the wfc has a capital B, while the **Checkbox** class in the awt has a lower case b.

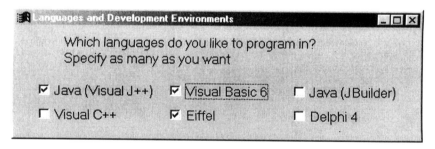

Fig 15.6 Using the CheckBox class.

The **RadioButton** class is used in a similar way except that radio buttons are grouped together within a container control, such as a **GroupBox**. Only one of the **RadioButton** objects can be checked. When another in the group is checked the others are automatically cleared. Fig 15.7 shows three groups of radio buttons, the lower two sets are contained within a **GroupBox** object. The text at the top of the **GroupBox** control is assigned by its **text** property. The top set use the form as their container. One common problem with checkboxes is that you must create the container control first and then add the radio buttons to it, creating them within the **GroupBox** control. If you create the radio button first then create the **GroupBox** control, Visual J++ will not recognize that the radio button is within the container control, and will use the form as the default container (assuming that the radio button is not created within another container.

You can set a **CheckBox** or **RadioButton** object or test its state using the methods shown in table 15.6.

Table 15.6 *Common properties of the **CheckBox** and **RadioButton** classes.*

Property	Description
boolean getChecked( )	Returns true if the control is checked or shaded.
int getCheckState( )	Returns the exact checked state of the control, **CheckState.CHECKED, INDETERMINATE** or **UNCHECKED**.
setChecked(boolean)	The boolean parameter sets or clears the control.
setCheckState(int)	Sets the exact state of the control.

The **RadioButton** and **CheckBox** classes, in common with other WFC controls can be enabled, making them available for use or disabled. In fig 15.7, if the *Summer* resort radio button is chosen the *Summer* group of radio buttons are enabled and the others are disabled. Similarly checking the *Winter* radio button makes only the *Winter* set of options available.

Fig 15.7 *Using the **RadioButton** class.*

The methods which handle the events which occurs when the checked status of the *Winter* or *Summer* radio buttons is changed are shown below:

```
private void radioButton2_checkedChanged(Object sender, Event e) {
// enable Summer options, disable Winter options
    if (radioButton2.getChecked( ))
    changeState(false, true);
}
```

```
private void radioButton1_checkedChanged(Object sender, Event e) {
// enable Winter options, disable Summer options
       if (radioButton1.getChecked())
   changeState(true, false);
   }

   public void changeState(boolean s1, boolean s2) {
       radioButton3.setEnabled(s1);
       radioButton4.setEnabled(s1);
       radioButton5.setEnabled(s1);
       radioButton6.setEnabled(s2);
       radioButton7.setEnabled(s2);
       radioButton8.setEnabled(s2);

   }
```

The **changeState** method is passed the new **enabled** statuses of the two groups of radio buttons and uses the **setEnabled** method to assign their new state.

The Panel class

The **Panel** class is the simplest of the container classes. They can be used to hold other controls such as radio buttons.

One of the more common uses is to use panels to improve the appearance of your forms, but dividing the area into differently coloured sections as shown in fig 15.8.

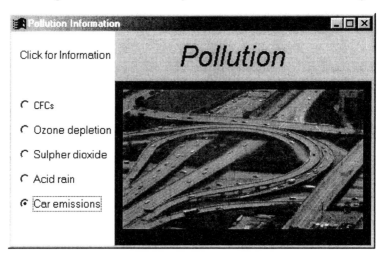

*Fig 15.8 Using the **Panel** class.*

The **backColor** property determines the panel colour.

The ComboBox Class

There are three types of **ComboBox** objects as shown in fig 15.9. This appearance and behaviour is determined by the value of the **style** property which can have one of three possible values, **Simple**, **Dropdown** or **Dropdownlist**.

- The simple combo box always has a list below an editable region where you can type your own text.
- The dropdown has an editable region and a dropdown list which appears when you click on the down pointing arrow.
- The dropdown list does not have an editable region, just a list which appears when you click on the arrow.

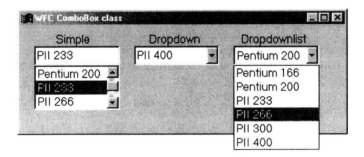

Fig 15.9 *Different styles of **ComboBox** objects.*

To add text at design time click on the **items** property which runs the String List Editor. Each line you type corresponds to an entry in the combo box.

The combo box is probably the most complex of the WFC controls to use, therefore in the next example we are going to see how you can use some of the most commonly used methods. In this application, shown running in fig 15.10, the combo box is initially empty.

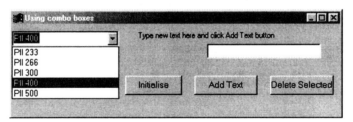

Fig 15.10 *Updating a **ComboBox** object at run time.*

When you click on the *Initialise* button, a list of items is added to the combo box using the **setItems** method, the **setStyle** method makes the combo box a dropdown type, and the **setSorted** method puts the entries in the combo box into alphabetical order. The **getItem** method returns the first item in the combo box (with an index of zero). This is converted into a string and displayed in the edit box at the top of the combo with the **setText** method.

The *Add Text* button adds the text typed into the edit control to the combo box using the **addItem** method. Note that **addItem** adds a single item to the combo box and **addItems** adds an array of items.

The *Delete Selected* button gets the index of the selected item using the **getSelectedIndex** method. The index returned is used in the **removeItems** method to delete the selected item from the combo box. The previous item in the list is displayed; however, if the item deleted was the first item, the **getItemCount** method is used to find the number of items in the combo box. The last item is displayed with the **setText** method. The first item in the combo box has an index of 0, the last item in a combo box which has x items will therefore have an index of x-1.

The code for this application is shown below:

```
public class Form1 extends Form {
    private void button1_click(Object sender, Event e) {
    // initialise the combo box
        String comboText[ ] = {"PII 233", "PII 266", "PII 300", "PII 400"};
    // Put the items in alphabetical order
        comboBox1.setSorted(true);
    // make it a dropdown combo
        comboBox1.setStyle(ComboBoxStyle.DROPDOWN);
    // add the items to the combo box
        comboBox1.setItems(comboText);
    //display the first item
        comboBox1.setText((comboBox1.getItem(0)).toString( ));
    }

    private void button2_click(Object sender, Event e) {
    // add the text typed into the edit control to the combo box
        comboBox1.addItem(edit1.getText( ));
    // display the new item added
        comboBox1.setText(edit1.getText( ));
    // clear the edit control
        edit1.setText("");
    }

    private void button3_click(Object sender, Event e) {
    // delete selected item
        int c = comboBox1.getSelectedIndex( );
    // if no item selected do nothing
        if (c >= 0) {
    // delete the selected item
            comboBox1.removeItem(c);
            c--;
    // display the previous item, if the first item
    // has been deleted, display the last item
                if (c < 0) c = comboBox1.getItemCount( ) - 1;
```

> *comboBox1.setText((comboBox1.getItem(c)).toString( ));*
> }
> }
> // *The Visual J++ generated code follows here*

There are a comprehensive set of methods for managing combo boxes as shown in table 15.7.

*Table 15.7 Methods of the **ComboBox** class.*

Property	Description
addItem(Object)	Adds a new item to the combo box and returns the index of the item.
getItem(int)	Returns the item at the specified index.
getItemCount( )	Returns the number of items in the combo box.
getItems( )	Returns all items in the combo box as an array of objects.
getSelectedIndex( )	Returns the index of the currently selected item.
getSelectedText( )	Returns the text of the currently selected items.
getSelectionEnd( )	Returns the index of the last selected item.
getSelectionStart( )	Returns the index of the first selected item.
setItem(int, Object)	Inserts the object at the specified index position.
setItems(Object[ ])	Initializes a combo box with the array of objects.
setSelectedIndex(int)	Selects the specified item.
setSelectedText(String)	Replaces the currently selected text with the specified text.
setSorted(boolean)	Specifies if the entries in the combo box are to be sorted or not.
setStyle(int)	This method controls the style of the combo box, which is either, **ComboBoxStyle.SIMPLE, DROPDOWNLIST** or **DROPDOWNLIST**.

The ListBox and CheckedListBox class

The behaviour of the **ListBox** and **CheckedListBox** classes is very similar to that of the **ComboBox** class. **CheckedListBox** is a subclass of **ListBox**.

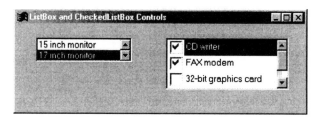

*Fig 15.11 The **ListBox** and **CheckedListBox** controls.*

There are some additional methods for the **CheckedListBox** which manage the check box aspects as shown in Table 15.8.

Table 15.8 *Methods of the **CheckedListBox** class.*

Property	Description
getCheckedIndices( )	Returns an array containing the indices of the checked items.
getItemCheck(int)	Returns a value which indicates the checked state of the specified item.
setItemCheck(int, int)	The parameters are the item number and the checked state of that item, use either **CheckState.CHECKED**, **PARTIAL** or **UNCHECKED**.

The HScrollBar and VScrollBar classes

Horizontal and vertical scrollbars have a **minimum** and **maximum** value which reflects the **value** of the slider. The amount of movement the slider makes when the arrow at the ends of the scrollbar is clicked is the **smallChange**. The movement when the space between the slider and the end arrow is clicked is the **largeChange**.

In the running application shown in fig 15.12, the maximum value for the horizontal scroll bar has been set to 100 while the minimum value remains at 0. The **smallChange** value is 2 and the **largeChange** value is 15. The default for **smallChange** is 1 and 10 for **largeChange**. New values have been assigned for the vertical scroll bar. The current value of position, returned by the **getValue** method, is shown in the associated edit boxes every time the slider moves.

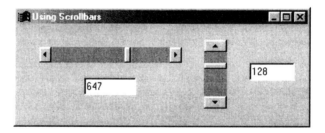

Fig 15.12 Horizontal and vertical scrollbars.

The code for this application is shown below:

```
public class Form1 extends Form
{
    private void Form1_paint(Object sender, PaintEvent e)
    {
    HScrollBar1.setLargeChange(15);
    HScrollBar1.setSmallChange(2);
    HScrollBar1.setMaximum(1000);
    VScrollBar1.setLargeChange(20);
    VScrollBar1.setSmallChange(4);
    VScrollBar1.setMinimum(100);
    VScrollBar1.setMaximum(200);
```

```
        }

        private void VScrollBar1_scroll(Object sender, ScrollEvent e)
        {
              edit2.setText(Integer.toString(VScrollBar1.getValue( )));

        }

        private void HScrollBar1_scroll(Object sender, ScrollEvent e)
        {
              edit1.setText(Integer.toString(HScrollBar1.getValue( )));
        }
// The Visual J++ generated code follows here
```

The PictureBox class

The **PictureBox** class is used to display images. The **image** property specifies the image which is displayed. If you select this property in the Properties window, you can browse for an image file, which can be any of the popular formats including bmp, gif and jpg, ico and emf.

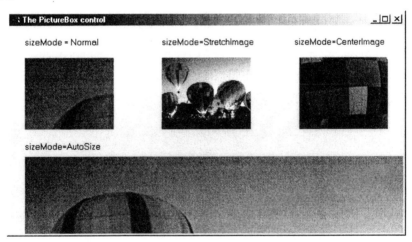

Fig 15.13 The sizeMode property of the PictureBox class.

The **sizeMode** property control some important aspects of how the image is displayed. It can be one of four values:

- **Stretch Image**. The size of the image will change so that it fits exactly the size of the control, if the control is resized the image is also resized.
- **Auto Size**. The size of the control is changed to fit the size of the image.

- **Normal.** Only the portion of the image which will fit into the control area is displayed. Neither the control nor the image are resized. If the image is smaller than the control it is displayed in the top left corner of the control.
- **Center Image.** The central part of the image is displayed. Neither the control nor image are resized.

You can change this property and others at run time. Some of the most commonly used methods are listed in table 15.9:

Table 15.9 *Methods of the **PictureBox** class.*

Name	Description
int getSizeMode( )	Returns an integer indicating if this property is either Normal(0), Stretch Image(1), Auto Size(2), or Center Image(3).
Bitmap getImage( )	Returns the current image.
setSizeMode(int)	Sets the state of the **sizeMode** property to one of the four possible values.
setImage(Image)	Assigns a new image to the control.

The Timer and TrackBar classes

The **Timer** control has an **interval** property which is the time in milliseconds between timer events. The **enabled** property must be set to true for these events to occur. The **Timer** control is not visible at runtime so its position does not matter. In the application shown in fig 15.14, the countdown time in seconds is specified in the edit box at the top of the application. When the button is clicked, the countdown starts and the position of the slider on the **TrackBar** control moves. When the countdown reaches zero the application ends. Note that the timer events continue to occur at the specified interval while the control is enabled.

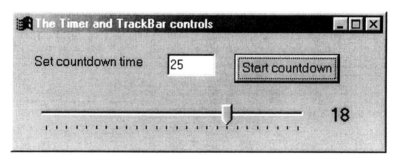

Fig 15.14 *The **Timer** and **TrackBar** controls.*

The **TrackBar** control behaves in a similar way to the scroll bar controls. The minimum and maximum values are determined by the **min** and **max** properties and the position of the slider by the **pos** property.

The code for the application is shown below:

```
private void Form1_paint(Object source, PaintEvent e) {
// set initial values for the timer and trackbar
    initialiseTimer(10);
// disable the timer
    timer1.setEnabled(false);
}

private void initialiseTimer(int time) {
// get the countdown time
    edit1.setText(String.valueOf(time));
// set the counter to the countdown time
    edit2.setText(edit1.getText( ));
// set the maximum and minimum values of the trackbar
    trackBar1.setMaximum(time);
    trackBar1.setMinimum(0);
// set the position of the trackbar to the countdown time
    trackBar1.setValue(time);
}
    private void button1_click(Object source, Event e) {
// set the countdown time to that typed
    initialiseTimer(Integer.parseInt(edit2.getText( )));
// the timer event will occur every 1000 milliseconds
    timer1.setInterval(1000);
// start the timer running
    timer1.setEnabled(true);
}
    private void timer1_timer(Object source, Event e) {
// the timer has expired
// get the current value displayed, convert to int and decrement
    int c = Integer.parseInt(edit1.getText( )) - 1;
// display the new time value
    edit1.setText(String.valueOf(c));
// move the trackbar slider to the new position
    trackBar1.setValue(c);
// if the countdown is zero, end the application
    if (c==0) System.exit(0);
}
// the Visual J++ generated code goes here
```

The properties of the **Timer** and **TrackBar** controls can be referenced and changed at run time by the methods shown in tables 15.10 and 15.11.

*Table 15.10 Methods of the **Timer** class.*

Name	Description
getInterval( )	Returns the interval between timer events in milliseconds.
setInterval(int)	Sets the interval between events to the specified value in milliseconds.

*Table 15.11 Methods of the **TrackBar** class.*

Name	Description
int getMinimum( )	Returns the value returned when the slider is in the minimum position.
int getMaximum( )	Returns the value returned when the slider is in the maximum position.
int getValue( )	Returns the current position of the slider.
setMinimum(int)	Sets the minimum to a new value.
setMaximum(int)	Sets the maximum to a new value.
setValue(int)	Sets the position of the slider to the specified value.

The MainMenu control

The final control we are going to look at is the **MainMenu** control. The position of this control does not matter since it is not visible at run time. This component greatly simplifies the process of creating complex menu systems. Add the control to the form in the usual way. On the menu bar you are prompted for the places that you can type a menu item as shown in fig 15.15. Menu items can be modified or deleted. To add a separator line use a single '-' character.

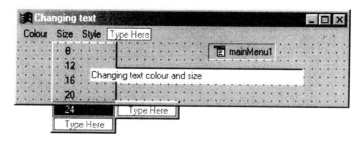

Fig 15.15 Creating menus.

The working application is shown in fig 15.16. The *Colour* menu changes the colour of the displayed text. The *Size* menu offers a range of different font sizes. The *Style* menu allows you to underline or italicize the text.

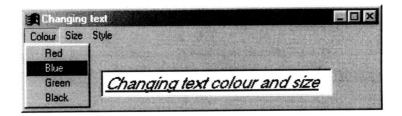

Fig 15.16 The running application.

To create the event procedure for a menu item double click on that item. The code for the application is shown below:

```
public class Form1 extends Form
{
        private void menuItem14_click(Object sender, Event e) {
        // change between underline and non underline
                edit1.setFont(new Font((edit1.getFont( )).getName( ),
                                        (edit1.getFont( )).getSize( ),
                                        (edit1.getFont( )).getUnits( ),
                                        (edit1.getFont( )).getWeight( ),
                                        (edit1.getFont( )).getItalic( ),
                                        !((edit1.getFont( )).getUnderline( )),
                                        (edit1.getFont( )).getStrikeout( )));
        }

        private void menuItem13_click(Object sender, Event e) {
        // change between italic and non italic
                edit1.setFont(new Font((edit1.getFont( )).getName( ),
                                        (edit1.getFont( )).getSize( ),
                                        (edit1.getFont( )).getUnits( ),
                                        (edit1.getFont( )).getWeight( ),
                                        !((edit1.getFont( )).getItalic( )),
                                        (edit1.getFont( )).getUnderline( ),
                                        (edit1.getFont( )).getStrikeout( )));
        }

        private void menuItem12_click(Object sender, Event e) {
        // set size to 24 point
                setSize(24);
        }
        private void menuItem11_click(Object sender, Event e) {
        // set size to 20 point
                setSize(20);
        }
        private void menuItem10_click(Object sender, Event e) {
        //set size to 16 point
                setSize(16);
```

```
        }
        private void menuItem9_click(Object sender, Event e) {
        //set size to 12 point
            setSize(12);
        }
        private void menuItem8_click(Object sender, Event e) {
        //set size to 8 point
            setSize(8);
        }
        private void setSize(int newSize) {
        // this method is called to change the font size
            edit1.setFont(new Font((edit1.getFont( )).getName( ),
                    newSize,
                    (edit1.getFont( )).getUnits( ),
                    (edit1.getFont( )).getWeight( ),
                    (edit1.getFont( )).getItalic( ),
                    (edit1.getFont( )).getUnderline( ),
                    (edit1.getFont( )).getStrikeout( )));
                    }

        private void menuItem7_click(Object sender, Event e) {
        // black
            edit1.setForeColor(Color.BLACK);
        }

        private void menuItem4_click(Object sender, Event e) {
        // red
            edit1.setForeColor(Color.RED);
        }

        private void menuItem6_click(Object sender, Event e) {
        // green
            edit1.setForeColor(Color.GREEN);
        }

        private void menuItem5_click(Object sender, Event e) {
        // blue
            edit1.setForeColor(Color.BLUE);
        }
// the Visual J++ generated code follows
```

Note that the **Color** class used is from the **wfc.ui** package and should not be confused with the **Color** class in the **java.awt** package. The behaviour and the names of the methods in these two classes are similar, but there are some differences that can cause problems, for example **Color.blue** is a **final static** variable (that is a constant) of the **java.awt.Color** class, while **Color.BLUE** is a **final static** variable of the **com.ms.wfc.ui.Color** class. The use of the **Color** class in the abstract windowing toolkit is covered in the next chapter.

16
The Graphics Class

Introduction

Virtually all of the best Web pages you have seen will have one thing in common, great graphics. Good graphics not only make your pages seem more interesting, but allow you to get information across more easily. In this chapter we are going to see how you can use Visual J++ to create and manipulate graphics in your applets.

The **Graphics** class provides an extensive set of methods for drawing simple graphics including lines, ellipses and rectangles. It also allows you to import existing images. Visual J++ has a set of tools so that you can create your own images or edit existing ones.

The co-ordinate system

Before we start creating graphical images we need to know about the co-ordinate system that Java uses.

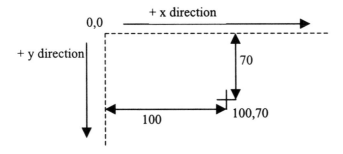

Fig 16.1 Java's co-ordinate system.

As shown in fig 16.1, the top left of the drawing area is the 0,0 position, with positive x co-ordinates extending to the right and positive y co-ordinates extending downwards. When specifying the co-ordinates of a point the x co-ordinate is always given first.

Drawing lines and text

The most commonly used methods in the **Graphics** class are used for writing text and for drawing simple lines:

- *drawString(String str, int x, int y).* Writes the text *str* at co-ordinates *x, y*.
- *drawLine(int x1, int y1, int x2, int y2).* Draws a line between *x1, y1* and *x2*, y2.

An example of using these two methods is shown below, with the output in fig 16.2:

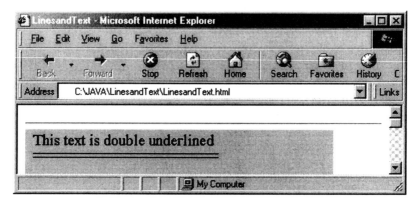

Fig 16.2 Drawing lines and text.

```
public void paint(Graphics g) {
    g.drawString("This text is double underlined", 10, 20);
    g.drawLine(10, 30, 180, 30);
    g.drawLine(10, 35, 180,35);
}
```

Later in this chapter we look at how you change the font, size and style of your text.

Drawing rectangles

There are a comprehensive set of methods for creating the most basic rectangular shape, offering filled, round cornered and 3D effect rectangles:

- *drawRect(int x, int y, int width, int height).* Draws a rectangle of the specified width and height. The top left corner is given by the x, y co-ordinates (assuming that the width and height are positive).
- *drawRoundRect(int x, int y, int width, int height, int arcWidth, int arcHeight).* Draws a rectangle with rounded corners.
- *draw3DRect(int x, int y, int width, int height, boolean raised).* Draws a rectangle with a raised 3D effect. If the boolean is **true** the effect is raised, if **false** it is lowered.
- *fillRect(int x, int y, int width, int height).* A filled rectangle.

- **fillRoundRect(int x, int y, int** width, **int** height, **int** arcWidth, **int** arcHeight). A filled round cornered rectangle.
- **fill3DRect(int x, int y, int** width, **int** height, boolean raised). A filled 3D effect rectangle.

Plain and 3D rectangles

The code below uses the **drawRect** and the **draw3DRect** with the raised boolean false in the centre rectangle and true in the right rectangle. The second row of rectangles are the corresponding filled forms:

```
public void paint(Graphics g) {
    int x = 10, y = 10, width = 50, height = 50;
    int arcWidth = 20, arcHeight = 20;
    g.drawRect(x, y, width, height);
    g.draw3DRect(x+60, y, width, height, false);
    g.draw3DRect(x+120, y, width, height, true);
    g.fillRect(x ,y+60, width, height);
    g.fill3DRect(x+60, y+60, width, height, false);
    g.fill3DRect(x+120, y+60, width, height, true);
}
```

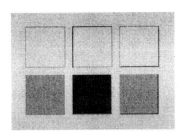

Fig 16.3 Drawing plain and filled rectangles.

The first comment is that all of the top row and all of the bottom row are virtually the same! This is because you cannot increase the line thickness and so to obtain a reasonable 3D effect, you need to draw several 3D rectangles one inside the other:

```
public void paint(Graphics g)
{
    int x = 10, y = 10, width = 50, height = 50;
    g.setColor(Color.green);
    for (int c=1; c<10; c++) {
        g.draw3DRect(x + c, y + c, width - c*2, height-c*2, false);
        g.draw3DRect(x + 60 + c, y + c, width - c*2, height-c*2, true);
        g.fill3DRect(x + 120 + c, y + c, width - c*2, height-c*2, false);
        g.fill3DRect(x + 180 + c, y + c, width - c*2, height-c*2, true);
```

```
        }
    }
```

This produces the rectangles shown in fig 16.4. Note that the *x* and *y* position increases by 1 every time the rectangle is drawn and the *width* and *height* decreases by 2, so that each rectangle drawn fits exactly inside the other.

Fig 16.4 Drawing 3D rectangles.

A more obvious 3D effect is obtained by changing the colour of the lines drawn using the **setColor** method, in this case to change the lines drawn to green. The **Color** class is covered later in this chapter.

Round cornered rectangles

The **drawRoundRect** and **fillRoundRect** methods use the same arguments as the corresponding **drawRect** and **fillRect** methods except for two additional arguments, *arcWidth* and *arcHeight* which define the degree of curvature.

The top left corner of the rectangle is shown in fig 16.5, indicating the significance of the *arcWidth* and *arcHeight* arguments.

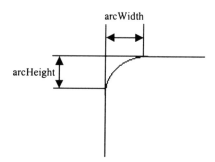

Fig 16.5 Drawing round cornered rectangles.

The method below draws a round cornered rectangle.

```
public void paint(Graphics g) {
    int x = 30, y = 30, width = 200, height = 200;
    int arcWidth = 80, arcHeight = 70;
    g.drawRoundRect(x, y, width, height, arcWidth, arcHeight);
}
```

Drawing polygons

Rectangles are a special form of the more generalized polygon drawing methods. There are two forms of the **drawPolygon** method and the corresponding **fillPolygon** method.

- *drawPolygon(int xPoints[ ], int yPoints[ ], int nPoints).*
- *fillPolygon(int xPoints[ ], int yPoints[ ], int nPoints).*
- *drawPolygon(Polygon p).*
- *fillPolygon(Polygon p).*

The first two methods requires three arguments:

- An array of x co-ordinates.
- An array of y co-ordinates.
- The number of pairs of x and y co-ordinates.

The following Java code produces the code displayed in fig 16.6:

```
public void paint(Graphics g) {
    int xPoints[ ] = {10,50,10,50,10,110,210,170,210,170,210};
    int yPoints[ ] = {150,130,110,90,70,50,70,90,110,130,150};
    int nPoints = xPoints.length;          // gives the number of co-ordinates
    g.drawPolygon(xPoints, yPoints, nPoints);
    for (int c=0; c< nPoints; c++ )
        xPoints[c] += 220;
    g.fillPolygon(xPoints, yPoints, nPoints);
}
```

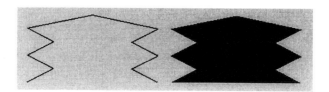

Fig 16.6 Drawing polygons.

To use the alternative **drawPolygon** method you need to create an object of the **Polygon** class and to use a constructor to insert the data points and the number of points. The following Java code produces exactly the same output as shown in fig 16.6.

```
public void paint(Graphics g)
{
    int xPoints[ ] = {10,50,10,50,10,110,210,170,210,170,210};
    int yPoints[ ] = {150,130,110,90,70,50,70,90,110,130,150};
    int nPoints = xPoints.length;
    Polygon p1 = new Polygon(xPoints, yPoints, nPoints);
    g.drawPolygon(p1);
    for (int c=0; c< nPoints; c++ )
        xPoints[c] += 220;
```

```
        Polygon p2 = new Polygon(xPoints, yPoints, nPoints);
        g.fillPolygon(p2);
}
```

Drawing ovals and arcs

Circles are just special forms of ovals with the width and height arguments the same. There are two methods:

- **drawOval(int x, int y, int width, int height)**
- **fillOval(int x, int y, int width, int height)**

The *x* and *y* arguments are the position of the top left corner of the smallest rectangle which would enclose the ellipse.

Arcs are a part of an oval. There are two methods:

- **drawArc(int x, int y, int width, int height, int startAngle, int arcAngle)**
- **fillArc(int x, int y, int width, int height, int startAngle, int arcAngle)**

The *x*, *y*, *width* and *height* values define a rectangle which could contain a complete oval. The *startAngle* and *arcAngle* values determine what portion of that oval is actually drawn.

In fig 16.7, the x and y values define the top left corner of the rectangle, the width and height values define the dimensions of the rectangle. The arc which is actually drawn is the bold part of the oval, between 90 and 180 degrees.

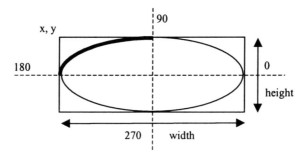

Fig 16.7 Drawing arcs.

The zero degree position is at 3 o'clock and anti-clockwise is the positive direction, so 90 degrees is at 12 o'clock. In fig 16.7, the starting position (the fifth argument) is 90 degrees. The arc drawn extends 90 degrees and so the sixth argument is also 90 degrees. A common mistake is to think that the final argument is the end position, rather than the number of degrees swept by the arc.

The Java code required to produce this arc is shown below:

```
    g.drawArc(10, 10, 150, 80, 90, 90);
```

The **fillArc** method creates pie shaped sections, filling in the area from the centre of the ellipse to the ends of the arc as shown in fig 16.8:

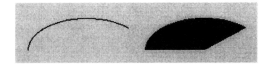

Fig 16.8 The drawArc and fillArc methods.

The code which produces this figure is:

g.drawArc(10, 10, 150, 80, 45, 135);
g.fillArc(160, 10, 150, 80, 45, 135);

Using colours

All of the drawing we have done so far is in the default colour, but you have complete control over the colours used in your applet. When designing Web pages it is important to remember that not every monitor used to run your applet will have access to the same range of colours. Therefore to ensure that your applet appears the same on all computers it is advisable to stick to a few standard colours as defined in the **Color** class in the **java.awt** package (do not confuse this class with the **Color** class in the **wfc.ui** package, which is used when you are creating Windows applications).

Table 16.1 The RGB values of the standard colours

Colour	Red	Green	Blue
Color.black	0	0	0
Color.blue	0	0	255
Color.cyan	0	255	255
Color.darkGray	64	64	64
Color.gray	128	128	128
Color.green	0	255	0
Color.lightGray	192	192	192
Color.magenta	255	0	255
Color.orange	255	200	0
Color.pink	255	175	175
Color.red	255	0	0
Color.white	255	255	255
Color.yellow	255	255	0

In Java, colours are defined using 24-bit RGB colour, that is 8-bits for each of the red, green and blue components. The **Color** class in the **java.awt** package defines a set of class variables representing the standard colours as shown in table 16.1.

It is useful to see what the red, green and blue components of the standard colours are if you cannot remember what colours cyan or magenta are.

You can also create your own colours using one of three constructors:

- **Color(int r, int g, int b)**. Each of the arguments is an integer value between 1 and 255 representing each of the components.
- **Color(float r, float g, float b)**. These arguments are float values between 0 and 1.
- **Color(int rgb)**. In this single integer argument, bits 16-23 represent the red component, bits 8-15 the green and bits 0-7 the blue.

For example, to create red colour with a touch of green and blue:

Color myColour = new Color(255, 20, 20);

Changing colours

If you want to change the current colour in which your graphics objects will be drawn use the **setColor** method of the **Graphics** class:

setColor(Color c);

In the example shown in fig 16.9, random ovals of random size are drawn in random positions in random colours!

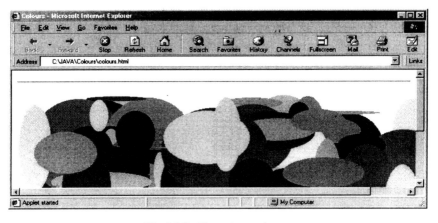

Fig 16.9 Changing colours.

The Java code is shown below:

```
public void paint(Graphics g) {
        int x, y, width, height;
        float red, green, blue;
        for (int c = 0; c < 100; c++) {
            x = (int)(Math.random( ) * 700);
            y= (int)(Math.random( ) * 200);
            width = (int)(Math.random( ) * 200);
            height = (int)(Math.random( ) * 200);
            red = (float)Math.random( );
            green = (float)Math.random( );
```

```
        blue = (float)Math.random( );
        g.setColor(new Color(red, green, blue));
        g.fillOval(x, y, width, height);
    }
}
```

Since **paint** is called every time the form is resized, a new set of randomly coloured filled ovals are redrawn whenever this happens.

If you are drawing shapes which are not filled, the current colour applies to the line used to draw these shapes.

You can change the colour of the drawing background itself, using the **setBackground** method:

```
    setBackground(Color c);
```

for example:

```
    setBackground(Color.white);
```

The **setBackground** method is a method of the **java.awt.Component** class which the **Applet** class inherits.

Working with fonts

If you want to display some text, the easiest way is to use the **drawString** method of the **Graphics** class. So far the examples we have looked at have used a default font, but you have complete control over the size, font and style of text displayed using the **Font** class. This is a part of the **java.awt** package.

The **Font** class has only one constructor which can be used to describe the initial properties of the **Font** object:

```
    public Font (String name, int style, int size);
```

- The name parameter is the name of the font.
- The style is either **Font.BOLD**, **Font.ITALIC** or **Font.PLAIN**.
- The size is the size of the font in points.

The applet shown below displays the text shown in fig 16.10. An array of three **Font** objects called *f* is created. For text to be displayed in this font, the **setFont** method of the **Graphics** class must be used.

```
import java.applet.*;
import java.awt.*;

public class Fonts extends Applet {
    public void paint(Graphics g) {
        Font[ ] f = new Font[3];
        f[0] = new Font("TimesRoman", Font.BOLD, 15);
        f[1] = new Font("Courier", Font.ITALIC, 20);
        f[2] = new Font("Helvetica", Font.PLAIN, 25);
```

```
for (int c = 0; c <3; c++){
    g.setFont(f[c]);
    String text = "This font is ";
    text += f[c].getSize( )+ " point " + f[c].getName( );
    int style = f[c].getStyle( );
    if (style == Font.BOLD) text += " BOLD"; else
        if (style == Font.ITALIC) text += " ITALIC"; else
        if (style == Font.PLAIN) text += " PLAIN";
    g.drawString(text, 10, 30 + c*30);
    }
}
}
```

You can create a font which is both italic and bold:

Font f = new Font("Courier", Font.BOLD + Font.ITALIC, 10);

You can combine **Font.PLAIN** with **Font.ITALIC** or **Font.BOLD**, but the addition of the **Font.PLAIN** style has no effect on the style used.

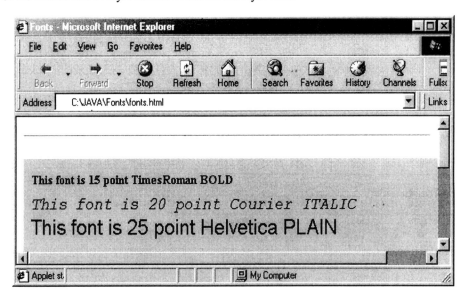

Fig 16.10 Changing fonts.

The **getSize** and **getStyle** methods of the **Font** class are used above, in addition there are some other useful methods of the **Font** class as shown in table 16.2.

Table 16.2 *The methods of the* **Font** *class in the* **java.awt** *package.*

Method	Description
boolean equals(Object)	Returns **true** if the supplied object is a **Font** object with the same name, style and size.
String getFamily( )	Returns the platform specific name of the font.
String getName( )	Returns the logical name of the font.
boolean toString( )	Returns a string which represents the properties of the current font.
boolean isBold( )	Returns **true** if the font is bold.
boolean isItalic( )	Returns **true** if the font is italic.
boolean isPlain( )	Returns **true** if the font is plain (not bold or italic).

Finding available fonts

One of the benefits of Java is that your applet or application can run on any platform, however this does cause some problems. If you are working solely in a PC environment you will have a very good idea of the available fonts, but if you are writing for a multi-platform environment you cannot make this assumption. The problem is made worse, since if you specify a non-existent font, the default font will be used instead (although it will have the specified style and size). It is therefore safest to stick to the most widely used fonts, virtually every computer system will have Times Roman and Courier fonts available, so if you want platform independence it is best to stick to these.

You can find out what fonts are available by using the **getFontList** method. This is a method of the **Toolkit** class which is an abstract superclass. The **getDefaultToolkit** method is a static method of this class which gets the default toolkit for the system and returns a **Toolkit** object. The **getFontList** method returns a list of the fonts as a **String** array.

The method shown displays two rows of text. The top row is a list of all of the fonts available. The bottom row is a list of the font names each written in that font.

```
public void paint(Graphics g) {
        String fonts[ ] = Toolkit.getDefaultToolkit( ).getFontList( );
        Font fStandard = new Font("TimesRoman", Font.PLAIN, 20);
        for (int c=0; c < fonts.length; c++) {
            g.setFont(fStandard);
//display font name in TimesRoman
            g.drawString(fonts[c],20 + c*110, 20);
            Font f = new Font(fonts[c], Font.PLAIN, 20);
            g.setFont(f);
//display the font name in that font
            g.drawString(fonts[c],20+ c*110, 40);
        }
}
```

The output of this applet is shown in fig 16.11.

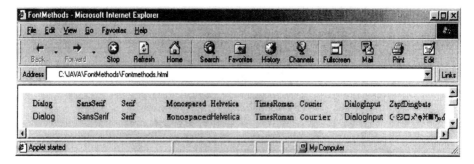

Fig 16.11 *Displaying available fonts.*

Using images

We have seen how you can create simple graphics using the methods of the **Graphics** class to draw lines and basic shapes. You can also incorporate your own images and use any of the graphics editors available on your system to open and modify these images:

- Select the **File | Open File** menu option.
- In the **Type of Files** list box, select the **Common Java Files** option.
- Browse through your files to select the file that you want to import.
- Click on **Open**.

If you have opened a BMP file, the image will be displayed as shown in fig 16.12 within the Windows Paint application.

Fig 16.12 *Editing images.*

If you have used any of the standard drawing packages such as CorelDraw, most of the features of this application will be familiar. The usual tools are supplied as shown in table 16.3. If you cannot see the graphics or colour toolbar select the appropriate option from the **View** menu.

Table 16.3   The Paint tools.

Tool	Description	Tool	Description
	Selects a rectangular area.		Selects an irregular area.
	Colour selection. Click over any colour to select it.		Erases parts of the image.
	Fills a same colour area with the foreground colour.		Magnifies the image.
	Pencil. Draws a freehand line 1 pixel thick.		Brush. Draws a thick freehand line.
	Airbrush effect.		Add text.

The text tool allows you to select the font style and size as well as specifying text to be displayed.

In addition to the tools shown there are a set of tools for drawing lines, ovals, rectangles, rounded rectangles in both outline and filled format and for changing colours.

Displaying images

When you have found the image you want and changed it to the required format, you can display it:

- Define an object of type **Image**.
- Get the image using one of the **getImage** methods.
- Use one of the four **drawImage** methods of the **Graphics** class to display the image.

The code shown below displays the image shown in fig 16.13.

```
import java.applet.*;
import java.awt.*;

public class UsingImages extends Applet {
Image skaters;
```

```
public void init( ) {
    skaters = getImage(getCodeBase( ),"Images/Skaters.bmp");
}
public void paint(Graphics g) {
    g.drawImage(skaters, 10, 10, 450, 300, this);
}
}
```

The first problem is that you must specify the location of the image in the **getImage** method. The **getCodeBase** method of the **Applet** class returns the URL (in this case a Windows folder) of the current applet. The second parameter specifies the name of the image file, in this case *skaters.bmp*, which is in a sub folder of the applet's folder called *Images*. The running application displaying the image is shown in fig 16.13.

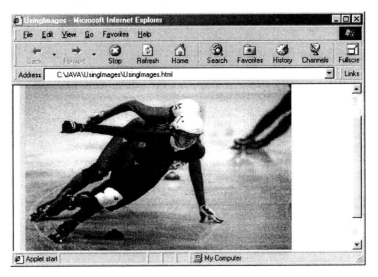

Fig 16.13 *An applet displaying an image.*

The following four overloaded **drawImage** methods have slightly varying functions:

- *drawImage(Image img, **int** x, **int** y, **ImageObserver** observer).*
- *drawImage(Image img, **int** x, **int** y, **Color** bgcolor, **ImageObserver** observer).*
- *drawImage(Image img, **int** x, **int** y, **int** width, **int** height, **Color** bgcolor, **ImageObserver** observer).*
- *drawImage(Image img, **int** x, **int** y, **int** width, **int** height, **ImageObserver** observer).*

All of the methods share the first 3 parameters, an object of type **Image**, and the x and y co-ordinates of the top left corner of the image.

The width and height parameters give the size of the image, which is stretched to fit rather than cropped.

The colour parameter specifies the background colour. Transparent pixels are drawn in this colour.

The final parameter is common to all methods, the **ImageObserver** object. This is used to monitor the image which is being loaded. In most cases **this** can be used.

There is a fifth overloaded method which has a different list of parameters:

- *drawImage(Image img, int dx1, int dy1, int dx2, int dy2, int sx1, int sy1, int sx2, int sy2, ImageObserver observer).*

The *dx* and *dy* parameters specify the co-ordinates of opposite corners of the destination rectangle. The *sx* and *sy* parameters specify the co-ordinates of opposite corners of part of the source image. The part of the source image specified is scaled to fit into the destination rectangle.

You can find the height and width of your image when you have loaded it by using the **getHeight** and **getWidth** methods of the **Image** class, both of these methods take an **ImageObserver** object as a parameter. In this case **this** can be used. If you wish, you can use these methods to ensure that the aspect ratio (the ratio of the height to width) is preserved or distorted as shown below:

```
import java.applet.*;
import java.awt.*;
public class DistortedImages extends Applet {
Image f;
    public void init( ) {
        f = getImage(getCodeBase( ),"Images/Runners.bmp");
    }
    public void paint(Graphics g) {
        g.drawImage(f, 10,10, f.getWidth(this)/4, f.getHeight(this)/4, this);
        g.drawImage(f, 10,150, f.getWidth(this)/3, f.getHeight(this)/6, this);
        g.drawImage(f, 300,40, f.getWidth(this)/6, f.getHeight(this)/4, this);
    }
}
```

This produces the images shown in fig 16.14.

Fig 16.14 Displaying distorted images.

17
Handling Exceptions

Introduction

Every application that we use or write is very likely to have bugs in it. More worrying is that even if we did have an application that did not have any errors we could not prove it. However thoroughly an application is tested it is usually impossible to check every combination of input data and circumstance which may arise, some of which are outside the control of the programmer. An unexpected situation, such as running out of memory is a contingency that few programmers are likely to have considered.

If you are able to anticipate that a problem may occur within your code, you can catch that error when it occurs and take some corrective action. You may, for example write an application which requests for the name of a file which it opens and reads. If you specify a non-existent file name it would be much better for your application to display a message such as *File not found* and to allow you to specify another file name, rather than simply crashing the application. Java provides a number of powerful, but simple methods which allow you to do this, and give you control over how problems are handled.

The Exception class

In Java an exception occurs when a program is unable to continue executing, but could recover if appropriate action is taken within the application. An exception occurs when Java executes a **throw** statement. Java will automatically execute a throw when an exception occurs, but you can include your own throw statement if you detect that an exception is imminent. When Java throws an exception, you can catch the exception with an exception handler, which takes some corrective action, even if it is only to report the problem.

Exceptions are members of the **Exception** class. Some of the more common exceptions of this extensive class hierarchy for the **java.lang, java.awt, java.io, java.net** and **java.util** packages are shown in fig 17.1. There are many more exceptions described in the on-line help for the other packages (especially the **ms.com.*** packages). You can also create your own exceptions, if the existing ones do not match closely enough the error condition you are trying to catch.

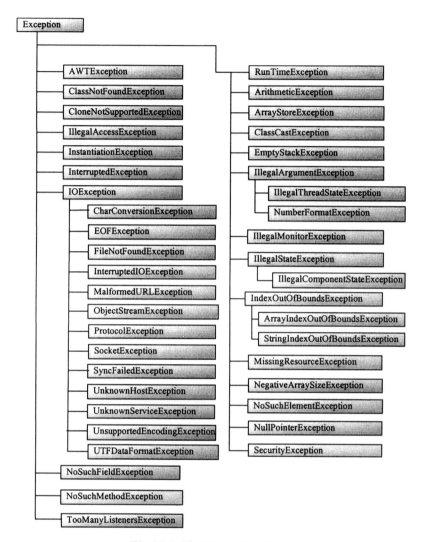

Fig 17.1 The Exception class.

Trying and catching

To catch a thrown exception, you enclose the code where the exception is likely to occur within a **try** clause. Immediately following this by a **catch** clause. When the exception occurs, control is passed to the **catch** clause which can take corrective action.

Fig 17.2 shows an applet in which two numbers are typed into the **TextField** components adjacent to the labels *First value* and *Second value*. When the button is clicked the two values are divided and the result displayed in the **TextField** with the **Label** *First/Second*. If the *Second value* is zero a divide by zero exception will occur.

and the name of the exception which has occurred **java.lang.ArithmeticException** is displayed at the bottom of the screen. In fig 17.2, a number with an invalid format has been typed and so the exception name, **java.lang.NumberFormatException** is displayed, followed by the invalid number.

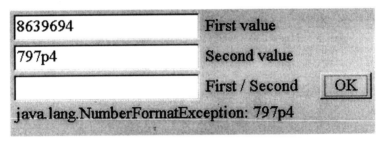

Fig 17.2 Catching an exception.

The **try** clause consists of the word **try** and brackets enclosing the code where the error may occur:

```
try {
    int top = Integer.parseInt(text1.getText( ));
    int bottom = Integer.parseInt(text2.getText( ));
    text3.setText(String.valueOf(top / bottom));
}
```

This is immediately followed by the **catch** clause, which has the name of the exception passed to it. In this case the **toString** method produces a string representation of the exception and uses the **setText** method to display the string in the **Label** *error*:

```
catch(Exception e) {
    error.setSize(400,20);
    error.setText(e.toString( ));
}
```

The complete applet is shown below:

```
import java.applet.*;
import java.awt.*;
import java.awt.event.*;
public class TryAndCatch extends Applet implements ActionListener {
    private TextField text1 = new TextField(20);
    private TextField text2 = new TextField(20);
    private Button ok = new Button(" OK ");
    private TextField text3 = new TextField(20);
    private Label error = new Label(" ");
    public TryAndCatch( ) {
        setFont(new Font("TimesRoman", Font.PLAIN, 20));
        setLayout(new FlowLayout(FlowLayout.LEFT));
        add(text1);
        add (new Label("First value      "));
```

```
            add(text2);
            add (new Label("Second value  "));
            add (text3);
            add (new Label("First / Second  "));
            add(ok);
            ok.addActionListener(this);
            add(error);
            }

    public void actionPerformed(ActionEvent evt)   {
            error.setText("");   //clear any error message
            try {
                    int top = Integer.parseInt(text1.getText( ));
                    int bottom = Integer.parseInt(text2.getText( ));
                    text3.setText(String.valueOf(top / bottom));
                    }
            catch(Exception e) {
                    error.setSize(400,20);
                    error.setText(e.toString( ));
                    }
            }
    }
```

Catching multiple exceptions

Sometimes there are a number of possible exceptions which may occur, and you may wish to take different action depending on the exception. We are going to modify the previous exception to treat the **NumberFormatException** differently from other exceptions. To do this we use multiple **catch** clauses. The new application is exactly the same as the previous one except that the single catch clause is replaced by the two clauses shown below:

```
catch(NumberFormatException e) {
        error.setSize(400,20);
        error.setText("Error in number format");
        }
catch(Exception e) {
        error.setSize(400,20);
        error.setText("Unspecified exception occurred");
        }
```

Since this code has separate exception handlers for the two exceptions you can take different action appropriate to the exception.

You cannot have a **catch** clause for an exception if it is preceded by a clause which catches an exception which is in its superclass. Exceptions which are lowest in the class hierarchy must come first. In particular, since all exceptions are subclasses of the **Exception** class the **catch** clause for the **Exception** class must come last. If you make a mistake in the order of your **catch** clauses, you will receive an error message when you build your application.

Creating new exceptions

If you want to throw an exception and the existing ones do not match your requirements, you can create your own, by creating a new class which extends an exception class which is closest to your exception. If, for example, you wanted to create an explicit *DivideByZero* class you would extend the **ArithmeticException** class:

```
public class DivideByZero extends ArithmeticException {
    public DivideByZero( ) {
        super("Division by Zero");
    }
}
```

The new class has one constructor with one line which calls the constructor for the **ArithmeticException** class passing it the string *Division by Zero*. Note that this is a **public** class and therefore cannot be in the same file as another **public** class.

Our new applet is identical to the previous one except for a slightly different **try** and **catch** clause. A check is made before the division occurs to see if a division by zero is about to occur, if it is, the *DivideByZero* exception is thrown. This is caught by a new **catch** clause for the *DivideByZero* exception class which we have created.

```
try {
    int top = Integer.parseInt(text1.getText( ));
    int bottom = Integer.parseInt(text2.getText( ));
    if (bottom == 0) throw new DivideByZero( );
    text3.setText(String.valueOf(top / bottom));
    }
catch(DivideByZero e) {
    error.setSize(400,20);
    error.setText(e.toString( ));
    }
```

The other two **catch** clauses follow as before.

The message displayed in the **catch** clause for the *DivideByZero* exception is the name of the exception followed by the text which was passed to the constructor for the **ArithmeticException** parent class in the constructor for the *DivideByZero* class. In this case the message is: *DivideByZero : Division by Zero*.

The finally block

If an exception occurs within a **try** clause, control is transferred to an appropriate **catch** clause. When the **catch** clause is completed, control leaves the method, however Java has a **finally** block which is always executed before a method is left, irrespective of whether an exception has occurred or not:

```
public class TryingAndCatching {
    public static void main(String[ ] args) {
        … … …
        try {
// If an error occurs in this try block, control
// will be transferred to the catch clause
            … … …
        }
        catch (Exception e) {
// since all exception classes are sub classes of Exception
// if an exception occurs in the try clause it is certain
// to come to this catch clause
            … … …
        }
        finally {
// this block is guaranteed to execute before the method
// is finished even if a return statement is executed
// elsewhere in the method
        }
    }
}
```

Throwing without catching

Sometimes an exception occurs which you do not want to handle in the method where it occurs. In this case you can just pass it up the line to the calling method. If no exception handling is found in that method it is up the line again and so on, until it finds a method which has a **catch** block which can handle the exception. In the worst case scenario, if you have not written a suitable catch handler, Java will handle the exception and display some error message before ending your program.

To throw exceptions from a method, list the exceptions which may be thrown at the start of the method:

```
void calculate (int one, int two) throws EOFException, FileNotFoundException {
    … … …
}
```

Although runtime exceptions can occur almost anywhere in a program, you do not have to throw **RunTimeException** or any of its subclasses from any method, these are implicitly included for you by Java.

18
The Visual J++
Debugger

Introduction

When you are designing complex applications you can anticipate some of the errors that may occur and deal with them using the exception handling techniques we have looked at. If, for example, you prompt for a file name and that file does not exist a **FileNotFoundException** is thrown that you can catch and request that another file name is specified. Sometimes, however, errors occur which are unexpected and the program crashes. Sometimes the program runs but produces unexpected results.

Visual J++ has a useful set of debugging tools which help you to examine the value of variables at different points in the execution of the program and so pinpoint the source of the problem.

In this chapter we are going to look at the different types of errors which can occur in a program and the tools which Visual J++ has to help you track down where errors occur.

Three types of errors

There are three different types of errors which can occur when you are writing programs:

- Compiler and linker errors.
- Runtime errors.
- Logic errors.

Each of these types of errors causes its own problems and there are different ways of dealing with them.

Compiler and linker errors

When you write a Java program, it must conform exactly to the formal specification of the Java language. Computer languages are designed to be completely unambiguous in their meaning, they do not have subtle shades of meaning like spoken human languages. A line of Java code is either syntactically correct or it is not. When you compile and link a program, its syntax is checked and also other features such as whether the parameter list of methods is correct. If a problem occurs at this stage, a compiler or linker error occurs. It means that your program does not conform to the Java language or that there are other problems such as using methods which are not available, or referring to variables which are out of scope. This type of error is usually the easiest to fix. Visual J++ reports on what the errors are and where they occur.

Runtime errors

If a program compiles and links correctly that does not mean that it will work correctly. If you run your application and it crashes unexpectedly this is a runtime error. It means that some situation has occurred in running the program which you did not consider and that the problem is so serious that the application cannot continue and crashes. If this occurs, Visual J++ will report on where the error occurred.

Logic errors

When a logic error occurs, the program may not crash but simply does not produce the expected answer. In this situation, there are two tools that you can use to find out where the problem is:

- You can stop the program at some point and examine the value of variables. Visual J++ also allows you to change the values of these variables without rebuilding and running your program again.
- You can step through your program a line at a time, examining variables at every stage.

Visual J++ offers flexible, refined versions of both of these tools.

Setting breakpoints

When your program does not produce the expected answers you will need to stop its execution at different points and examine the intermediate value of variables and follow the flow through the program. Programs can be broken in two ways:

- If you want to stop at a single point, you can move the cursor to the point you want to stop at and select the **Debug** | **Run to Cursor** menu option.

- If you want to stop at more than one point, move the cursor to the position where you want the breakpoint and right click to reveal the speed menu shown on the left of fig 18.1. Select the **Insert Breakpoint** option.

Fig 18.1 *Speed menu for lines with and without breakpoints.*

If you display the speed menu on a line where there is already a breakpoint the speed menu on the right of fig 18.1 is shown. Breakpoints are indicated by a filled circle on the left of the line of code. Sometimes you may wish to temporarily disable a breakpoint, you can choose **Disable Breakpoint** from the speed menu (this is only shown for lines which already have a breakpoint). A disabled breakpoint is shown by an empty circle on the left of the code. You can enable a breakpoint by selecting the **Enable Breakpoint** speed menu option, which is only displayed for lines which have a disabled breakpoint.

You can also manage your breakpoints using the **Debug** menu, which has options for inserting, enabling, disabling and clearing breakpoints, the menu displayed is slightly different dependent on whether the current line has a breakpoint and whether it is enabled or disabled. The **Debug | Breakpoints** option displays a dialog which can be used for management of the breakpoints as shown in fig 18.2.

Clicking on a checkbox in the **Breakpoints** box enables or disables the breakpoint. You can use the buttons to enable, disable, clear or remove one or more selected breakpoints.

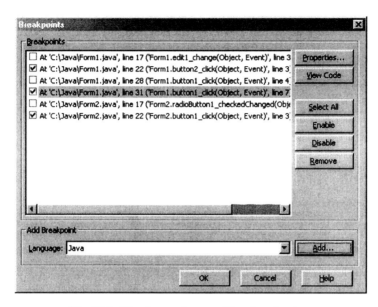

Fig 18.2 Viewing and controlling breakpoints.

Assigning conditions to breakpoints

Sometimes you may want a breakpoint to occur when a particular condition is met, or when a particular line of code has been executed a certain number of times.

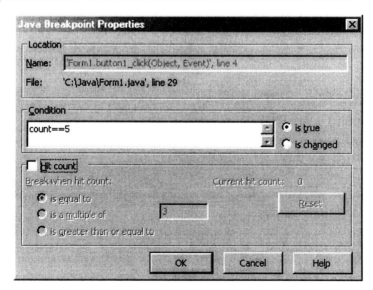

Fig 18.3 Setting conditions on breakpoints.

To display the Java Breakpoint properties dialog as shown in fig 18.3, click on the **Properties** button in the Debug dialog shown in fig 18.2.

If a fault only occurred after a line had been executed one thousand times it would be very tedious to break continue every time that number of times. Fortunately the debugger has the ability to break when a specified condition has been met or when a breakpoint has been encountered a specified number of times.

In the example shown, the breakpoint will pause execution of the program when the variable *count* is equal to 5. Alternatively you can also specify a **Hit count**. Every time the line is executed the **Hit count** increases by 1. The **Hit count** causes the application to pause whenever any one of the following three conditions (specified by radio buttons on the dialog) are met:

- The **Hit count** is reached.
- The **Hit count** is a multiple of a specified number (for example, you can break every third time).
- The **Hit count** is reached or exceeded.

What happens at breakpoints?

If you have breakpoints in your program and wish to run it ignoring the breakpoints; choose the **Debug | Start without Debugging** menu option, if you wish your breakpoints to be executed choose the **Debug | Start** button. Most people find it more convenient to display the Debug toolbar using the **View | Toolbars | Debug** menu option and to click on the icon as shown in fig 18.5.

When the program reaches a breakpoint it stops running as shown in fig 18.4. The breakpoints are clearly identified by the filled circle on the left of the lines of code, while the breakpoint the program is currently stopped at has a right pointing arrow in the centre of the filled circle. You can view and change the value of variables when the program pauses. The easiest way to see the value of a variable is simply to move the cursor over the variable name, its current value appears in a pop-up window. Unfortunately this does not work for object variables or arrays, and does not allow you to change the value of variables. You will need to be able to see the Locals and the Watch windows to do this. If these are not visible when your program stops at the first breakpoint select the **View | Debug Windows | Locals** and the **View | Debug Windows | Watch** menu options.

The Locals window displays the name, value and type of all local variables. Object variables or arrays have a plus sign adjacent to them. You can see all of the members by clicking on this icon. To collapse the tree click on the minus sign. You can change the value of a variable by double clicking on it and typing the new value in the value column.

The Watch window displays the name, value and type of variables that you specify. You do this by typing the name in the variable or expression. It is only updated when the program execution is stopped. You can change a value in the same way as for the Locals window, by double clicking on it and typing the value. You can also enter or delete values whenever the program is paused.

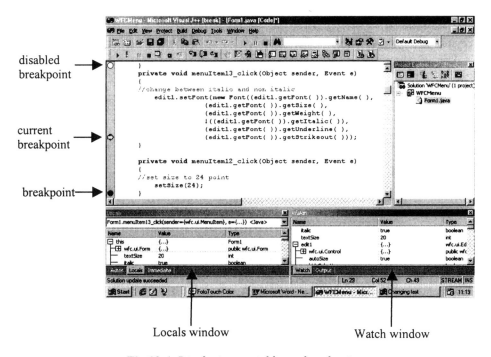

breakpoint ───►

current
breakpoint ───►

breakpoint ───►

Locals window   Watch window

Fig 18.4 Displaying variables at breakpoints.

Leaving a breakpoint

When you have examined the variables you want and perhaps changed their values, you can make your program continue in a variety of ways using the **Debug** menu options:

- The **Debug | Continue** option ends the debugging session and continues executing the application.
- **Debug | Restart** starts executing the program from the beginning.
- **Run to Cursor**. The program runs to the position of the cursor. The current cursor position is in effect given a temporary breakpoint.
- **End** closes the application.

Sometimes it is helpful to step through your program, pausing after the execution of a line or method. There are three menu options on the **Debug** menu to help you do this:

- **Step Into**. Executes the next line of code. If this is a method call, the program moves to the first line of the new method and breaks.
- **Step Over**. If the next line of code is a method call, the whole of the method is executed as if it were a single line of code.
- **Step Out**. If the current breakpoint is in a method, the program continues to the line after where the method was called.

All of these options are available from the Debug toolbar shown in fig 18.5.

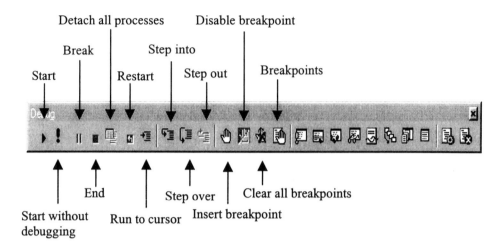

Fig 18.5 *The Debug toolbar.*

19
Using Files

Introduction

If you want to write an application that reads or generates large amounts of information, that data will be stored in one or more files. If you are writing applications that will run on a single computer or a network with a known file system, this is a common situation, and Java is only one of many languages that you could use. If you are writing applets, however, your program could be run on any computer with an unknown organisation of files. Browsers place restrictions on applets and prevent access to local files since it is too easy to contract a virus this way. A Web page entitled *Free Money!* would be sure to attract a lot of viewers. If it contained an applet which wrote a deadly virus to the disk it could have serious consequences for the thousands of people who would contract it. For this reason all of the examples in this chapter are applications.

We are going to look at the **System** class which handles basic input/output to the screen and the **InputStream** and **OutputStream** classes and their subclasses which allow you to read and write information to a file system.

The System class

When your application starts you have three public static I/O objects:

- **System.in,** this object is a member of the **BufferedInputStream** class and reads information from the keyboard.
- **System.out,** this is a **PrintStream** object and sends output to the screen.
- **System.err,** this is also a **PrintStream** object which outputs errors usually to the screen.

We have already seen the **System.out** object in use, but let us see how it can be used in conjunction with the **System.in** object.

You need to **import java.io.*** and to enclose the input/output code within a **try catch** clause. If an **IOException** occurs, the **catch** clause displays an error message and the name of the exception.

*Fig 19.1 Using **System.in** and **System.out**.*

The output from the application is shown in fig 19.1. This application prompts for your name. The response you type is read into a byte array:

System.out.print("What is your name : ");
System.in.read(b);

The **BufferedInputStream** class does not have a method which will read a string. The **read** method gets a byte array, if you attempt to display the byte array you have read:

System.out.println("Hello " + b);

The text shown is not what you have typed as shown in the second line of text displayed in fig 19.1. If you want to display the text correctly (as shown in the third line), you need to convert the byte array into a string first:

String name = new String(b,0);   // set the high byte to zero
System.out.println("Hello " + name);

In Java each character is stored in 2 bytes, the **String** class constructor used sets the high byte of each character to zero. The running application is shown in fig 19.1.

The complete application is shown below:

```
import java.io.*;
public class SystemIO {
    public static void main(String args[]) {
        byte b[] = new byte[50];
        try{
            System.out.print("What is your name : ");
            System.in.read(b);
// try to print Hello followed by the byte array
            System.out.println("Hello " + b);
// convert the byte array to a string and print Hello and that string
            String name = new String(b,0);  // set the high byte to zero
            System.out.println("Hello " + name);
            } catch (IOException e) {
            System.out.println("I/O error - " + e.toString());
        }
    }
}
```

The InputStream and OutputStream classes

Input and output is achieved by creating instances of subclasses of the abstract classes **InputStream** and **OutputStream,** shown in fig 19.2.

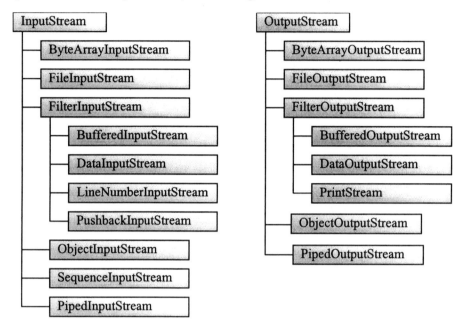

*Fig 19.2 The **InputStream** and **OutputStream** class hierarchy.*

File input/output requires instances of the **FileInputStream** and **FileOutputStream** classes, and it is these classes we are going to look at first.

Copying a file

In the next application we are going to open a text file and copy it a byte at a time to an output file. To read a file, create an instance of the **FileInputStream** class. The most widely used constructor for this class accepts the name of an existing file as a parameter:

>*FileInputStream input = new FileInputStream("input.txt");*

If the file does not exist, the exception **FileNotFoundException** is thrown.

To open a file for output, create an instance of the **FileOutputStream** class and specify the name of the output file to its constructor:

>*FileOutputStream output = new FileOutputStream("output.txt");*

If the specified file does not exist, one is created. If the file does exist, all of the existing data in it is erased. It is currently not possible to open a sequential file and append data to the end of it.

To read the data from the file, the **read** method is used. This is written to the output file using the **write** method:

```
b = input.read( );
if (b > 0) output.write(b);
```

The **read** method returns an integer read or −1 if the end of the file is reached.

All of the input/output must be placed within a **try** clause and have a corresponding **catch** clause. All the **catch** clause does in this application is to display an error message containing the name of the exception caught:

```
catch(Exception e) {
        System.out.println("Exception error  -  " + e.toString( ));
}
```

The complete listing of the application is shown below:

```
import java.awt.*;
import java.io.*;
public class CopyingFiles {
    public static void main(String args[ ]) {
        int b;
        try {
            FileInputStream input = new FileInputStream("input.txt");
            FileOutputStream output = new FileOutputStream("output.txt");
            do {
                b = input.read( );
                if (b > 0) output.write(b);
            } while (b > 0);
        } catch(Exception e) {
            System.out.println("Exception error  -  " + e.toString( ));
        }
    }
}
```

The **FileInputStream** and **FileOutputStream** classes are adequate for simple applications, but where you need to be able to read and write more complex data than a simple byte stream you need to use another class which has additional methods defined. The most commonly used classes are the **DataOutputStream** and the **DataInputStream** classes which are subclasses of the **FilterOutputStream** and **FilterInputStream** classes.

The FilterOutputStream class

This class overrides all the methods of the **OutputStream** superclass. It is the superclass of three classes which each provide additional functionality to existing streams:

- **BufferedOutputStream.**

- **DataOutputStream.**
- **PrintStream.**

We are going to look at each of these classes.

The BufferedOutputStream class

This class can output bytes to a stream. It is the companion class to the **BufferedInputStream** class. Bytes written using this class go into a buffer and when the buffer is full, the data is actually written to the underlying stream. The **flush** method empties the buffer, as does closing the stream.

The DataOutputStream class

Computer systems generally support two types of files systems; sequential files, which are opened and then read from start to finish and random access files, where you can read the data in the file in any order. The application shown in fig 19.3 prompts for a name and an address and writes that information to a sequential file when you click on the button. The text fields are erased and you can then enter another person's details. You can add as many records as you want, one of the records I have entered is shown in fig 19.3.

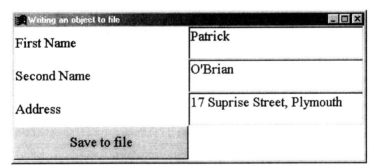

Fig 19.3 *Writing to a file.*

The **java.awt** and the **java.io** and **java.awt.event** packages need to be imported:

```
import java.awt.*;
import java.io.*;
import java.awt.event.*;
```

The components for the frame are defined as instance variables of the *OutToFile* class which extends the **Frame** class. The **main** method creates an instance of this class:

```
public static void main(String args[ ]) {
    OutToFile f = new OutToFile( );
}
```

The identifier *out* is defined as being a member of the **DataOutputStream** class:

DataOutputStream out;

In the constructor for the *OutToFile* class, these components are added to the frame (using the **add** method), the layout manager is changed to **GridLayout** (using the **setLayout** method), it is resized (the **setSize** method) and then the frame is displayed (the **setVisible** method).

The **FileOutputStream** class provides very limited functionality, it has three write methods all of which can only write bytes or arrays of bytes to the file. Most applications need to write the primitive Java data types to file, therefore it is usual to create an instance of the **DataOutputStream** class which has such methods.

```
try {
    out = new DataOutputStream(new FileOutputStream("People.txt"));
} catch (IOException e) {
    System.err.println("Cannot open file");
    System.exit(1);
}
```

The **FileOutputStream** class constructor is passed the name of the file to be opened. This instance of the **FileOutputStream** class is passed to a constructor for the **DataOutputStream** class. Opening a file can produce **IOException**. This exception is trapped by the **catch** clause.

When the button is clicked the **actionPerformed** method is called:

```
public void actionPerformed(ActionEvent e) {
// the button has been clicked, so write to file and clear fields
    addToFile();
    clearForInput();
}
```

Two methods are called, *addToFile* which writes the information typed in the text boxes to file and *clearForInput* which erases the text in the text fields. The text typed in the three text field can be accessed using the **getText** method. This is written to the file in UTF-8 encoding by the **writeUTF** method. UTF-8 writes first the number of bytes in the string, followed by the string itself.

```
private void addToFile() {
    try{
        out.writeUTF(firstName.getText());
        out.writeUTF(secondName.getText());
        out.writeUTF(address.getText());
    } catch(IOException e) {
        System.err.println("Error writing to file");
        System.exit(1);
    }
}
```

A **try** and **catch** clause is needed in case there is an error writing to file. Finally an inner class is added which extends the **WindowAdapter** class and closes the application when the close icon in the top right corner of the frame is clicked. If it is, the application is terminated:

```
public class Close extends WindowAdapter {
// handles the clicking of the window's close icon
    public void windowClosing(WindowEvent e) {
        System.exit(0);
    }
} //end of the Close class
```

The complete application is shown below:

```
import java.awt.*;
import java.io.*;
import java.awt.event.*;

public class OutToFile extends Frame implements ActionListener {

    TextField firstName = new TextField(20);
    TextField secondName = new TextField(20);
    TextArea address = new TextArea(3,30);
    Button ok = new Button(" Save to file ");
    DataOutputStream out;

    public OutToFile( ) {
        setTitle("Writing an object to file");
        setFont(new Font("TimesRoman", Font.PLAIN, 20));
        setLayout(new GridLayout(4,2));
        add(new Label("First Name"));
        add(firstName);
        add(new Label("Second Name"));
        add(secondName);
        add(new Label("Address"));
        add(address);
        add(ok);
        // add a listener for the button
        ok.addActionListener(this);
        setSize(350,300);
        setVisible(true);
        // add a listener for the clicking of the window's close icon
        addWindowListener(new Close( ));
        try {
            out = new DataOutputStream(new FileOutputStream("People.txt"));
        }
        catch (IOException e) {
            System.err.println("Cannot open file");
            System.exit(1);
        }
    }
```

```
public class Close extends WindowAdapter {
// handles the clicking of the window's close icon
    public void windowClosing(WindowEvent e) {
        System.exit(0);
    }
} //end of the Close class

public void actionPerformed(ActionEvent e) {
// the button has been clicked, so write to file and clear fields
    addToFile( );
    clearForInput( );
    }

private void clearForInput( ) {
    firstName.setText("");
    secondName.setText("");
    address.setText("");
}

private void addToFile( ) {
    try{
        out.writeUTF(firstName.getText( ));
        out.writeUTF(secondName.getText( ));
        out.writeUTF(address.getText( ));
        }
    catch(IOException e) {
        System.err.println("Error writing to file");
        System.exit(1);
        }
    }

public static void main(String args[ ]) {
    OutToFile f = new OutToFile( );
    }
}
```

In addition to the methods defined in the **OutputStream** class for writing to a file and the useful **writeUTF** method, there are numerous methods which write the primitive Java data types to file as shown in table 19.1:

Table 19.1 *Methods of the **DataOutputStream** class.*

Method	Method
writeBoolean(boolean)	writeDouble(double)
writeByte(int)	writeFloat(float)
writeBytes(String)	writeInt(int)
writeChar(int)	write(long)
writeChars(String)	write(short)

The PrintStream class

The **PrintStream** class provides a convenient way of writing data which is not in the form of bytes. We have already used this class implicitly for displaying text in an application:

System.out.println("This uses the PrintStream class");

This class has an extensive set of overloaded **print** and **println** methods for writing the basic Java types such as characters and integers as well as strings and objects.

The FilterInputStream class

This class overrides all the methods of the **InputStream** superclass. It is the superclass of four classes which each provide additional functionality to existing streams:

- **BufferedInputStream.**
- **DataInputStream.**
- **LineNumberInputStream.**
- **PushbackInputStream.**

We are going to look at each of these.

The BufferedInputStream class

The **BufferedInputStream** class allows you to read from an input stream where the data is read ahead in blocks, therefore when a request is made for more bytes the information may already be available from the buffer. When the buffer is empty a read request causes another block to be read. Buffering cannot be seen by the application user, but it can give great improvements in performance, particularly if the data is being read from a disk file which has an access time measured in milliseconds compared to nanoseconds for memory. This class can only read byte streams.

The DataInputStream class

We are going to read the file which we wrote in the previous example. This file should contain several records, one of the records I have entered is shown in fig 19.4.

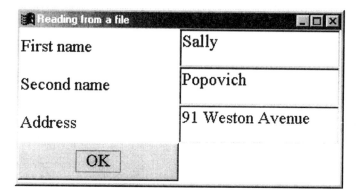

Fig 19.4 Reading from a file.

This reading application is similar in many ways to the writing application. The identifier *in* is defined as an instance of the **DataInputStream** class:

> *DataInputStream in;*

The constructor from this class is called when *in* is instantiated and the file *people.txt* is specified:

> *in = new DataInputStream(new FileInputStream("People.txt"));*

When the button is clicked the **actionPerformed** method is called which reads the information from the file using the **readUTF** method and displays it in the corresponding text fields using the **setText** method.

```
public void actionPerformed(ActionEvent e) {
    // the button has been clicked, so read from the file
    try{
        firstName.setText(in.readUTF());
        secondName.setText(in.readUTF());
        address.setText(in.readUTF());
    }
    catch(EOFException eofEvent) {        //end of file - take no action
    }
    catch(IOException ioEvent) {
        System.err.println("Error reading from file");
        System.exit(1);
    }
}
```

The exceptions which may be thrown by these input/output methods require a **try** and two **catch** clauses. The complete program listing is shown below:

```
import java.awt.*;
import java.io.*;
import java.awt.event.*;

public class InFromFile extends Frame implements ActionListener {

    TextField firstName = new TextField(30);
    TextField secondName = new TextField(30);
    TextField address = new TextField(20);
    Button ok = new Button(" OK ");
    DataInputStream in;

    public InFromFile( ) {
        setTitle("Reading from a file");
        setFont(new Font("TimesRoman", Font.PLAIN, 20));
        setLayout(new GridLayout(4,2));
        add(new Label("First name "));
        add(firstName);
        add(new Label("Second name"));
        add(secondName);
        add(new Label("Address"));
        add(address);
        add(ok);
        // add a listener for the button
        ok.addActionListener(this);
        setSize(350,300);
        setVisible(true);
        // add a listener for clicking the window's close icon
        addWindowListener(new Close( ));
        try {
            in = new DataInputStream(new FileInputStream("People.txt"));
        } catch (IOException e) {
            System.err.println("Cannot open file");
            System.exit(1);
        }
    }

    public class Close extends WindowAdapter {
        // handles the clicking of the window's close icon
        public void windowClosing(WindowEvent e) {
            System.exit(0);
        }
    }// end of Close class

    public void actionPerformed(ActionEvent e) {
```

```
        // the button has been clicked, so read from the file
        try{
                firstName.setText(in.readUTF( ));
                secondName.setText(in.readUTF( ));
                address.setText(in.readUTF( ));
                }
        catch(EOFException eofEvent) {          //end of file - take no action
                }
        catch(IOException ioEvent) {
                System.err.println("Error reading from file");
                System.exit(1);
                }
        }
}


        public static void main(String args[ ]) {
                InFromFile f = new InFromFile( );
        }
}
```

In addition to the **readUTF** method, the **DataInputStream** class has an extensive set of methods for reading from files, some of which are listed in table 19.2:

Table 19.2 *Methods of the **DataInputStream** class.*

Method	Description
boolean readBoolean( )	int readInt( )
byte readByte( )	long readLong( )
char readChar( )	short readShort( )
double readDouble( )	int readUnsignedByte( )
float readFloat( )	int readUnsignedShort( )

The LineNumberInputStream class

This class can only read byte streams, but offers the additional functionality of being able to count the number of lines read. A line is terminated by either a carriage return ('\r'), a newline character ('\n') or by a carriage return followed by a newline. The first line has a line number of zero.

The **getLineNumber** method returns an integer value giving the current line number. The **setLineNumber(int)** method resets the line number to the specified value.

The PushbackInputStream class

This class can only read byte streams, its unique feature is that it has a one byte pushback buffer. When the **unread(int)** method is used the byte is unread, that is the file pointer is moved backwards so that the next byte to be read is the one which was unread. The integer parameter of the **unread** method specifies the character to be pushed back.

Initially this seems to be strange functionality, but it does have a useful function. It is used when a sequence of bytes is terminated by a particular byte. When this terminating byte is read, the **unread** method can reposition the stream read pointer so that the next character to be read is that character, which is an indicator that the end of a sequence has been reached, rather than a part of the data itself.

20
Creating Database Applications

Introduction

Many real-world applications for the Windows environment use one of the many relational databases such as Microsoft Access. IDEs such as Visual Basic, Visual C++ and Borland's Delphi assume that this is going to be an important area for software developers and include a comprehensive set of tools and wizards. This is one of the reasons for their increased popularity. This version of Visual J++ incorporates many of these facilities, which will be familiar to many Windows programmers.

In this chapter we are going to look at the Data Forms Wizard which is the easiest way of creating an application which uses a relational database.

The Data Forms Wizard

The Data Forms Wizard allows you to create applications which use databases, but cannot create its own databases, therefore in this chapter we have used an existing database created with Access.

To create the database application:

- Select the **File | New Project** menu option and display the **New** page.
- Select the **Applications** folder.
- Select the **Application Wizard**, specify the name of your project and its location.
- Click on the **Open** button.

The form shown in fig 20.1 is displayed.

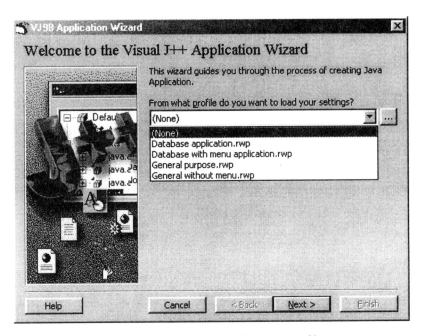

Fig 20.1 Choosing the application profile.

Choose the profile you want, the default is **(None)**. Click on **Next** to display the next form shown in fig 20.2.

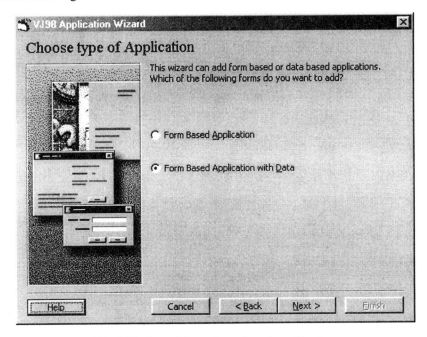

Fig 20.2 Specifying a form based application.

Select the **Form Based Application with Data** option, this will run the Data Form
Wizard.

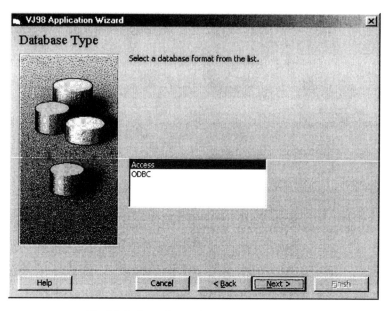

Fig 20.3 Specifying the type of database.

In this example, if your database is written in Access choose that option. Click on
Next to proceed.

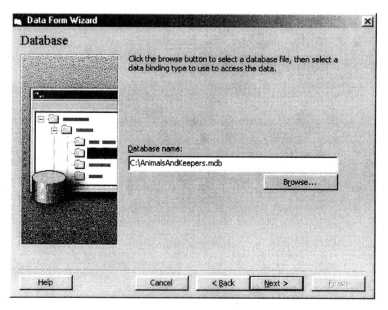

Fig 20.4 Specifying the database.

To specify the name of the database, you can browse through your file system if you wish to find it. Click on **Next** to proceed.

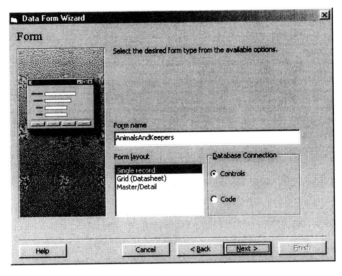

Fig 20.5 Specifying the layout of the form.

The layout of the form which will be created for your application is chosen in this option shown in fig 20.5. Click on **Next** to proceed.

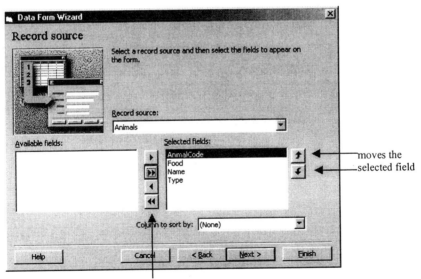

Moves fields between **Available** and **Selected**

Fig 20.6 Specifying the fields to be displayed.

Fig 20.6 shows that the **Record source** chosen is the table called *Animals* in the *AnimalsAndKeepers* database specified earlier. All of the fields in this database are listed in the **Available fields** edit box. For the completed application to display a field it must be moved to the **Selected fields** edit box. To move between these boxes, the two buttons with single buttons move the currently selected field. The buttons with two arrows move all of the components from one edit box to another. You can control the order of the selected fields by clicking the buttons with the up or down arrows. The currently selected field is moved. In this example all of the available fields are selected. Click on **Next** to proceed.

The next form shown in fig 20.7 displays the possible controls which can be added to the application.

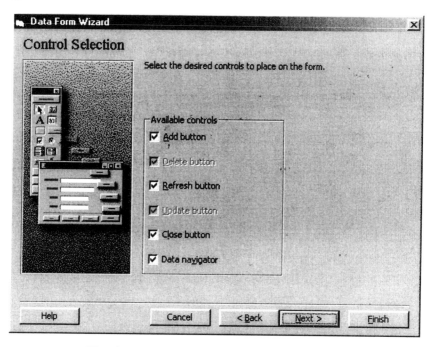

Fig 20.7 Specifying the controls to be displayed.

In this example all of the available options were chosen.
The **DataNavigator** is a WFC control which allows you to move to:

- The next record.
- The previous record.
- The first record. If the first record is displayed no action is taken.
- The last record. If the last record is currently displayed no action is taken.

Click on the **Next** button to proceed.

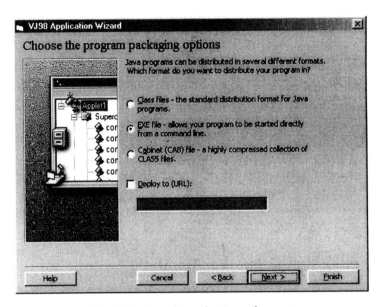

Fig 20.8 Specifying the type of output.

As for all Windows-based applications you can choose the type of output. The default is **EXE file**. Click on **Next** to proceed. The final window asks you if you want to save the choices you have made as a profile as discussed in chapter 14, and gives you the choice of displaying a summary, which is shown in fig 20.9.

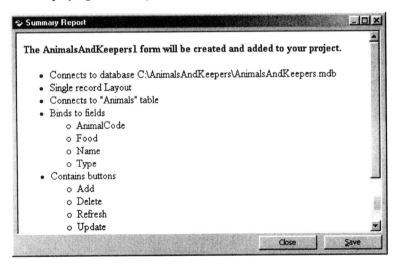

Fig 20.9 The summary report.

Click on the **Close** button in the summary report and then select the **Finish** button to end the wizard. The completed application at design time is shown in fig 20.10.

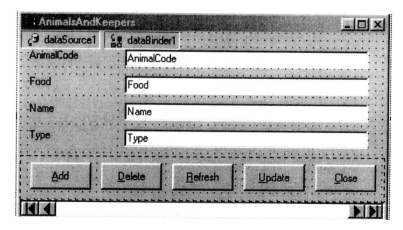

Fig 20.10 *The application at design time.*

The application can be modified and controls moved or added in the usual way. The running application is shown in fig 20.11.

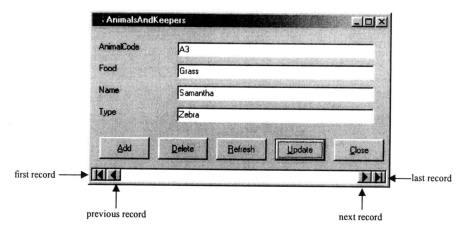

Fig 20.11 *The running application.*

The data navigator is at the bottom of the form in fig 20.11 and is used to browse through the database.

Index